THAT WOMAN I MARRIED: MARRIAGE AND THE FAMILY

by
Melvin R. Miller

EPWORTH METHODIST CHURCH
HOPE VALLEY ROAD
DURHAM, NORTH CAROLINA

THAT WOMAN I MARRIED: MARRIAGE AND THE FAMILY

by
Melvin R. Miller

Unless otherwise indicated, all scripture quotations are taken from *The King James Version* of the Bible.

Scriptures so indicated are taken from *THE HOLY BIBLE: Revised Standard Version.* Copyright © Old Testament Section 1952, New Testament Section 1946, by the Division of Christian Education of the National Council of the Churches of Christ in the United States; Reference and Concordance Section 1959, by Thomas Nelson & Sons, New York.

THAT WOMAN I MARRIED: Marriage and the Family
ISBN 0-88144-061-2
Copyright © 1986 by Melvin R. Miller
Wesley Manor
Apt. #E-20
Jacksonville, FL 32223

Printed in the United States of America.
All rights reserved under International Copyright Law.
Contents and/or cover may not be reproduced in whole or in part in any form without the express written consent of the author.

Dedicated to

Bonnie Ruth,
my loving wife of 55 years.

PREFACE

Why another publication on the subject of marriage and family life when so many books and other massive material have already been formulated and published? Why . . . Because of the absence of certain basic and essential elements, principles, and truth; the foundation upon which all of the more effective and successful literature is based, but which has not seemed to have been recognized, understood, and identified by the writers and publishers of this mass of material.

My desire and purpose is to share with you how a minister, armed forces chaplain, and counselor came to discover the essential and basic elements of the foundation for effective and successful marriage and family life. Additionally, I wish to identify clearly and explain thoroughly the essential element, principle, and truth that I have learned in plain and simple terms understandable to an average sixth-grade student, and yet so profound as to command the intellectual and undivided attention of a person with a doctorate degree on the subject of marriage and family life.

Because the basic principle and material herein is unique to the marriage and family life subject (because marriage, itself, is unique within the human experience) and some of the ideas and facts that I present do, at times, cut 180° across much of the published material on the subject, I fully realize this work will not be an easy undertaking.

I am a retired United Methodist minister, a retired military chaplain, and a counselor. I have tried to write for the average layperson, with the hope the professionals in the field of marriage and the family (professors in institutions of higher learning, ministers, teachers, counselors, and lawyers) will digest and USE the concepts set forth in this book, because they DO WORK — 100% — when understood and FULLY executed by any married couple. They are based on the Holy Bible (Spiritual Laws) and "human nature" (natural laws of survival; which are known and used by every human being, animal, fowl, fish and insect). They are universally effective because God and "human nature" never change. I have found them to be understandable by and applicable to all human beings in the marriage relationship, regardless of their nationality, race, color, culture, creed, education, social standing, or sex.

I wish to thank my Heavenly Father, my wife, Bonnie Ruth, and the many married couples (who shared with me their deepest feelings of sorrow, pain, and heartache of their marital problems, to which many weary hours we struggled to find solutions and workable answers), each of whom has contributed to my understanding and knowledge of the marriage relationship. I also extend my gratitude to Reverend James Caroll Tollett, professor of theology at Oral Roberts University, for reading my material and encouraging its publication. And special thanks to Mrs. Melanie Ann Tollett for her dedicated and countless hours of tirelessly organizing, typing, and editing this manuscript.

TABLE OF CONTENTS

Chapter	Page
1. "That Woman" — "That Man"	9
2. Marriage is Unique, But Not Mysterious	13
3. A Unique Solution	21
4. Validity of Sound Counsel	27
5. That Memorable Day	33
6. The Research Begins	39
7. Defense Mechanisms	45
8. Relationships	53
9. Defense Mechanisms In Relationships	59
10. Cause of Wife and Husband Abuse	65
11. Marriage Creates and Takes Away	73
12. The Answer	77
13. Creative Ideas	85
14. The Two Are Now Made One	89
15. Another Phase	97

Chapter One
"That Woman" —
"That Man"

Why is it that whether you have lived with "that woman" to whom you have been married three days or thirty years, you still do not know how to handle her or you do not know what to do with her? Because she does not act or react like any other woman you have ever known. She does not act or react like your mother, your sister, your girl friends — in fact, she does not act or react like she did before you and she said "I do" in the marriage ceremony.

She seems to do so many things just arbitrarily, without rhyme or reason. You can't MAKE her do anything, and if you attempt or try to, you only start a family fuss, fight, pout, flood of tears, etc. You cannot even handle her now like you did before marriage, or like you do other women — your mother, sister, girl friend, or any other woman you have known. She is just "that woman" who acts the way she does because she wants to — she does not seem to want to do what is best or right. She does not want to listen to reason, be considerate, be agreeable, or cooperate. She only wants her own way. That is just the way "that woman" is.

Now, Madam, whether you are a "liberated woman," married, single, or divorced, please don't leave me yet, BECAUSE "that woman" with whom I have lived for over 55 years, the woman who is the mother of my four children, solemnly and firmly declares that all I have said above equally and fully —

100%+ — APPLIES TO ME. I am "that man" she married, and has lived with, these 55 years. So let us, together, continue our search for the truth of the matter. Thus, what I say from personal experience about "that woman," let us agree (and I am sure you will agree) that it applies fully — 100% — to "that man" to whom you are married. Hence, as you read, you just substitute he or him or man wherever it is appropriate. Then, think with me on the problem and look for the answer and solution. Yes, I can assure you there is an answer, because after being married more than 20 years, my wife and I found it.

Now, back to the question: Why is it that this woman can affect you as she does? Why is it that "this woman" is the only woman in the whole wide world whom you cannot handle or with whom you do not know what to do? (Whether this is the first time you have been married, or if you have been married before, the former wife still affected you the same way.) She is the ONLY woman in the whole wide world who can, in effect, leave you with the feeling of standing in the middle of the floor as if your feet were nailed down, your hands were tied to your sides, your mouth was taped closed, and a little blue blaze was coming out of the top of your head. "That woman" can and does affect you that way. Why and how can she do so?

No other woman can affect me like that. Why and how does "that woman" affect me like she does? Is there a logical, reasonable, and practical answer to this question? Yes, there is an answer and I have found it. Just stay with me and read on. I will tell you, in plain, simple, and understandable words what the answer is. This is a promise. I will not say maybe, I guess so, or this should work. I will tell you from hard experience that I know the answer — the solution — and I can assure you from personal experience it will work. Also, it can be used by any couple. This assurance, too, comes from practical experience of over 25 years of marital counseling and using the principles and explanation that I will set forth herein.

Yes, I know the answer. I had to know the answer for myself, after a simple incident occurred on a Saturday, about noon, when I came home to lunch from my office with some salvaged flowers from the discarded altar flowers from the chapel to make room for fresh ones for Sunday services. The details I will give you later. After that Saturday, I had to know why "that woman" affected me as no other women in the world had, or could. I had to know why. A little over 20 years earlier, I had married a beautiful young, healthy, vivacious, well-bred, well-mannered, educated, fifth- and sixth-grade school teacher. Although I had lived with "this woman," the mother of my four children, over 20 years, I had not discovered that she was "my wife." She was, therefore, not like my mother, my sisters, or my girl friends. In these 20 years, I had not known the role of a wife was a new and unique (no other known to the human race like it) human relationship, created by the marriage ceremony. I did not know "that woman" acted as she did because she was my wife. I did not know what a "wife" was, much less how one alters and rearranges life.

I was totally surprised to discover and learn "that woman" with whom I was living was having the same struggle with me — that cooperative, giving and forgiving, ever-loving, perfect husband of hers. You are probably surprised to learn that you, too, are just "that man" who will not act or react like any other man she has ever known, such as her father, brother, boy friend, and that you do not even act as you did before the wedding. Now, are you surprised to discover that you, too, can leave "that woman you married," in effect, standing in the middle of the floor with a helpless feeling as if her feet were nailed to the floor, her hands were tied to her sides, her mouth was taped shut, and a blue blaze was coming out of the top of her head? Well, you — that perfectly properly behaving and ever-loving husband — can and do affect the little woman you affectionately and publicly call "my wife," that way.

"Me?" you say. "I do? Why? How? I am really trying to be a good husband."

No doubt she, too, is trying hard to be a good wife . . . but . . . well . . . there just seems to be something you do not understand and are not doing right. You just cannot understand what makes "that woman" tick, what she wants, what she is trying to do, why she acts — well — so arbitrarily, sometimes without rhyme or reason. I will, I repeat, give you the answer that I found for myself. Just be patient and stay with me. You will learn how simple, yet profound, understandable, and effective our discourses have been for more than 30 years, when we have shared ourselves with each other.

Chapter Two
Marriage is Unique, But Not Mysterious

If I can help you find satisfactory answers to all these questions of why and how, you will then have discovered the basic principles upon which marriage is founded. We will, together, have discovered the "framework" and "mode of operation" of marriage. We will have discovered and understood that marriage is, indeed, a unique human relationship.

The experience of marriage is unique, but not mysterious. Marriage is unique because there is no other human relationship like it. Many influences are brought to play on the human "will" in marriage choice by traditions of tribal, family, or political arrangement of a marriage, but the basic marriage creation is of the human will.

The wedding, or marriage relationship, is not created by physical location or the environment wherein one happens to reside, either by choice, chance, or circumstance. Environment can have an influence on becoming interested in or falling in love with another person and deciding to choose to marry an individual. However, your human will — choice — actually culminated the marriage relationship, regardless of the outside influences or pressures from tribe, family, political advantage, physical location, or environment.

Even the environmental situation of a woman and a man sharing the same house, table, bed, etc. does not create the marriage relationship. Some time ago, I was participating in a seminar on marriage and the family. When a case from a well-known author's book was brought up by one of the groups of participants, it was pointed out that this man and woman had lived together for a little over three years. They had gotten along very well. Hence, after living together for more than three years, they decided to get married. However, they lived together, after the marriage, just a little less than a year before they were divorced. Our group simply could not understand (even the professional counselor conducting the seminar did not have an answer) how this couple got along so well for over three years, but broke up with a divorce in less than one year after marriage.

This case is a classic illustration of the uniqueness of the marriage relationship. The couple in this case had lived together more than three years — they were not married. But when they took the marriage vows and in the true marriage relationship set up a home, that marriage relationship, being unique, required a different method, principle, and set of rules of operation than had existed before.

Marriage is the most unique relationship known to human beings. There is none other like it in all the existing relationships on this earth. However, marriage is not mysterious because the marriage experience can be explained and understood.

Marriage was ordained (intended to be) by the same force that created and brought about a male and a female in the human race. However, marriages are created by a man and a woman here on earth, not in some mystical place. Marriages put together or created under the laws of the Creator cannot be put asunder or destroyed by man. For our purpose in this book, we shall identify this Creative Mind that produced a man and a woman as "God." Hence, God created man in his own image, in the image of God created he him; male and female created he them. The basic marital law of the Creator is Genesis 2:24.

Through the years, I have more than once read Genesis 2:24 (KJV), "Therefore shall a man leave his father and his mother, and shall cleave unto his wife: and they shall be one flesh." I had also read, at least as many times, the expanded quotation of this verse by Jesus as recorded in Matthew 19:4-6, "Have ye not read, that he which made them at the beginning made them male and female, and said, For this cause shall a man leave father and mother, and shall cleave to his wife; and they twain shall be one flesh? Wherefore they are no more twain, but one flesh. What therefore God hath joined together, let not man put asunder." I have also read, just as often, the Genesis tribute by Jesus in Mark 10:6-9, "But from the beginning of the creation God made them male and female. For this cause shall a man leave his father and mother, and cleave to his wife; and they twain shall be one flesh: so then they are no more twain, but one flesh. What therefore God hath joined together, let not man put asunder."

I had read all these scriptures with little concern and, perhaps, with less understanding, not really questioning the meaning of how "the two shall become one." I accepted without question the mystical union ideal expressed in the marriage ritual that I used in performing the marriage ceremony. However, this union is not mysterious, as described in the ritual of the marriage ceremony that we Methodists use: ". . . to join together this man and this woman in holy matrimony; which is an honorable estate, instituted of God and signifying unto us the *mystical union which exists* between Christ and his Church" (*Book of Worship*, United Methodist Church, p. 28, emphasis mine). The Church apparently took this clue from the Apostle Paul of the Bible's New Testament when, in Ephesians 5:28-33 (Revised Standard Version), he refers to marriage as "a great mystery." Paul told the Ephesians:

> Even so husbands should love their wives as their own bodies. He who loves his wife loves himself. For no man ever hates his own flesh, but nourishes and cherishes it, as Christ does the church, because we are members of his body. "For this reason a man shall leave his father and mother and be joined to his wife, and the two shall become one." This is a *great mystery,* and *I take it to mean Christ and the church;* however, let each one of you love his wife as himself, and let the wife see that she respects her husband.

The Apostle Paul, like the Psalmist, did not seem to understand Genesis 2:24. Maybe that is why Paul did not have a wife.

For so many years, I had blindly and naively accepted the Methodist marriage ritual concept as "the mystical union" of a man and a woman. I had not so much as noticed that St. Paul, after quoting Genesis 2:24, had plainly told the Ephesian Church that he did not understand or know what it meant. Paul said of the idea of a man and woman becoming husband and wife in marriage so that the "two shall become one" was, in fact, "a great mystery" to him. Paul said that he took this to mean the relationship between Christ and the Church.

Clearly, Paul did not recognize the Genesis 2:24 passage to refer literally to a flesh and blood man and woman through actual marital relationships to be joined as one, which Jesus very clearly said they do become in His quotation and explanation as recorded both in

Matthew and Mark. Definitely, marriage is unique — there is no other human experience comparable to it. However, it is not mysterious. The statement in Genesis literally means what it says; when a male and female (man and woman) are joined as husband and wife, "they become one." As the Genesis statement is explained by Jesus, ". . . he which made them at the beginning made them male and female, . . . For this reason shall a man . . . be joined to his wife: and the two shall become one . . . . So they are no longer two, but one." How? There is a real and understandable answer.

When we understand why it is that we cannot handle a wife or a husband as we do other women or men, that she or he is "that woman" or "that man" and can affect us as no other living man or woman can, then we shall also be able to understand what Jesus meant when he was questioned about His stand on marriage and divorce in his day, as recorded in Matthew 19:3-8 and Mark 10:4-8.

When Jesus was asked, "Is it lawful for a man to divorce his wife?" His counter-question was, "What did Moses tell you?" To this, the leaders answered, "Moses allowed a man to write a certificate of divorcement, and put her away." In Matthew 19:8, Jesus then responded "For your hardness of heart Moses allowed you to divorce your wives, but from the beginning it was not so." Mark 10:6-8 quotes Jesus as saying:

> But from the beginning of creation, "God made them male and female." For this reason a man shall leave his father and mother and be joined to his wife, and the two shall become one. So they are no longer two but one. What therefore God hath joined together, let not man put asunder.

When, therefore, we find the answer to our seeming inability to deal satisfactorily with our marriage partner or mate (to be discussed in greater detail later), we will discover, as was inferred by Jesus in the beginning, divorce was not inherent in the very creation of man and woman. We will discover that divorce today could be non-existent, because it is not inherent or an integral part of marriage. Therefore, if the principles of the marriage relationship are properly understood and exercised, divorce would not, in fact could not, become a reality because the "two would be one" and, hence, inseparable. There could be no such process or thing as a divorce — marriage would be inseparable if "the two were one."

When we have discovered the basic principles of the why and the how of marriage behavior, we will understand the meaning of "The two shall be one," which philosophy, reason, and mathematics would all say is a literal impossibility, and which theology and the Church has called a mystery. But we shall see that two becoming one not only can, but must, be an actual and literal fact and the concept is understandable, reasonable, and, therefore, no mystery. When understood, this basic principle of marriage becomes everyday common sense; practiced in all other fields of endeavor and behavior. We could — if we understood and exercised the principal of "two becoming one" in marriage — end this writing here (as many childhood storybooks used to say of the Prince and the Princess) with "and they lived happily ever after."

This basic principle is an understandable, reasonable, psychological, and mathmatical fact; it can be comprehended and practiced by any normal adult, regardless of nationality, race, creed, social standing, sex, education, or material possessions. In fact, the basic principles governing marriage can be understood by the average school child, because these basic principles upon which a successful marriage depends are the same ones employed by the school child in his or her everyday living and behavior toward other people — toward classmates, teacher, brother, sister, mother, father, etc.

Marriage is not a 50-50 proposition. I used to say this was true, but I have found that when each of us comes half way, we have only created a "head-on collision." Marriage is also unique in that it is the only mathematical equation in life where 50% + 50% will not equal 100% — it takes at least 60% + 60% (that extra 10%) to make a 100% complete marriage. When each partner has at least a 10% overlap, it creates an embrace — not a collision — and it is pretty difficult to fight when you are embracing each other.

Marriage is unique — there is no other human experience like it. However, marriage is not mysterious. The marriage relationship can be both explained and understood. Anything that can be explained and understood by the average human mind surely is not a mystery. Marriage can be explained in simple enough terms for an average sixth-grade student to understand it, yet challenge the undivided intellectual attention of someone holding an earned Ph.D.

I fully realize the above statements have raised many questions, promised much, and sound almost dogmatic in their thesis. But for more than 30 years, having employed and tested this basic philosophy and thesis in "pre-marital counseling" and "family counseling" (which are treated alike, using exactly the same material, with no difference, for what "fits" for making a successful marriage will also "fit" for holding a marriage together, or bind it together when it is breaking apart), the successful results obtained have completely convinced me of its merit and value.

Chapter Three
A Unique Solution

For over a quarter of a century, these have been the kinds of responses I have had from this marriage and family counseling. But the strange thing to me is that through the years, I have searched diligently and have found no one, or any published literature on marriage and the family using or even recognizing the existence of these God-given inherent, simple, basic, elementary, and dynamic principles of marriage and family relationship that I have discovered, and for over a quarter of a century have been using with such effective results.

Having studied in four leading universities, four well-known schools of theology, and one of the foremost foundations on marriage and the family in the United States, to my amazement and disappointment I found none of these seemed to be even aware of, much less using or teaching, the simple rules of the basic principles upon which marriage is founded and efficiently functions.

For over 40 years, I attended and participated in study groups, special classes, conferences, and seminars on "Marriage and Family Life." These were endorsed, sponsored, and/or conducted by well-known institutions: Colleges, Universities, Schools of Theology, Ministerial Associations, and the Chaplain's Service of the United States Air Force. At other times, these sessions were under such religious organizations and denominations as: Lutherans, Episcopalians, Presbyterians, Baptists, Congregationalists, Disciples of

Christ, Church of God, Nazarenes, Judaism, Roman Catholics, and United Methodists. Still others were run by: Perkins School of Theology, Southern Methodist University, Bangor School of Theology, Southeastern Baptist Theological Seminary, and the internationally recognized Hogg Foundation on Marriage and Family Life at the University of Texas.

Through these groups, classes, seminars, conferences, and other sessions, I did acquire many stimulating ideas, methods, experiences, and a mass of information, much of which was useful and helped make me a more effective marriage and family life counselor. However, at the conclusion of each study group, class, seminar, conference, private personal conference, or casual conversation with many of my teachers, professors, and professional marriage counselors or fellow ministers and armed forces chaplains, I still had a deep and haunting feeling there was something more. I felt there were some pertinent, basic, and absolutely "I-must-know" elements that we were all missing — unanswered questions. As a husband of more than 20 years (at that time) and the father of three lively children, I did not even know the questions to ask, much less the answers to that which was so deeply disturbing and haunting to me.

In these institutions of learning, much good to excellent material was taught and published, but the basic principles and understanding of marriage were not taught in the classroom, nor were they in the published literature in their libraries, neither have I found it in dozens of libraries I have researched. However, one of the concepts taught to me by some of these institutions was that "Inherent in the marriage relationship is the element of conflict." My knowledge

A Unique Solution

and experience in the field demanded me to reject this idea. This is true in every human and even animal relationship EXCEPT marriage. Herein lies the uniqueness of marriage, which the Psalmist of the Holy Bible and apparently other modern teachers and authors do not yet seem to have discovered, although it has been known and even in written history for thousands of years (you can find the basic statement of principal recorded in the Holy Bible, Genesis 2:24). This is what so amazes and puzzles me. Why have the authorities of education and religious leaders and counselors not discovered the meaning of the concept stated here? Why was I so long in discovering these truths which I had read so many times? I believe in my findings; they are sound, factual, basic, and revolutionary, yet so simple and basic to everyday life and living that a sixth-grade school child can understand them, yet can command the undivided intellectual attention of someone with a doctoral degree.

I had not yet come to recognize that marriage was an experience unique in human relationships. Nor had I been challenged to ask why and how the marriage relationship was unique to all other experience and relationships and, therefore, could not successfully be dealt with or handled in the same way as other human relationship. Most assuredly, I had not the most remote idea or concept of the necessity of a different approach, understanding, basic principle, method, or rule for marital relationships, than those that we all use from the cradle to the grave to deal with, handle, solve, or just cope with all our other human experiences and relationships. I did not know the two "defense mechanisms" that we all use (as do all living creatures), to a more or less successful degree, to deal with life's problems and stay alive were not valid to handle the marriage relationship. These two universally used "defense mechanisms" of avoidance and force cannot, to any degree, be successfully used in dealing with, handling, solving, or coping with the marital relationship experience and/or marital problems. Marriage requires a different set of rules and processes.

Marriage is a unique human relationship because it is the one and only relationship known to and experienced by human beings that is not brought about or created by nature, that is, by birth or environment. The unique creative basis and essential element in the marriage relationship is the human will. Marriage is a "human choice" creation. Certain civilizations and cultural practices may influence the freedom of the individual's choice, but in the final analysis, human will creates the marriage. Marriage is unique, but not mysterious.

If the knowledge and understanding of what marriage really is during courtship, before marriage, does not influence, change, or stop the choice of a particular person as a chosen mate, then the understanding and full execution by both husband and wife, after marriage, of the principles set forth in the above cited scriptures, "the two shall become one," will surely hold the marriage together "till death us do part." Therefore, the marriage could not end in a divorce, but would last as was intended "from the beginning of creation."

Thus, I learned through years of hard work, personal experience, and through others sharing their marital problems and experiences with me as a teacher, pastor, armed forces chaplain, and marriage counselor, and through Divine guidance (because I do not believe

I possess the disposition and ability to discover this truth through my own effort alone) that Genesis 2:24, Matthew 19:4-6, and Mark 10:6-9 are literal and valid statements of truth regarding a living and literal marriage of a man and a woman. This truth can be explained and defended by the sciences of mathematics, psychology, philosophy, sociology, and just plain common sense and reason.

For several years, I have felt the Good Lord allowed me to stumble onto, and entrusted me with, some understanding of the basic principles of marriage, not seeming to be generally understood or practiced by either the ordinary man and woman in their day to day marital living or the professionals and experts in the field of marriage and the family. (In Luke 10:21, Jesus said God "hid these things from the wise and prudent and hast revealed them unto babes." I guess that is the way that I received it.) Hence, for several years, I have felt responsible, and even very guilty, for not sharing these findings with the rest of the world, because the home is basic to our civilization, culture, and very survival as a nation. The "rifts" in the American homes seem to be widening year by year. I feel the weakened home is the basis for much of our social strife and upheaval, moral breakdowns, riots, lack of respect and acceptance by child and parent of each other, not only in the United States, but in all nations and in all races. Therefore, I have finally decided to try to make public my thoughts and findings of more than 30 years of research and marital counseling experience.

Chapter Four
Validity of Sound Counsel

I have never had a couple with marital difficulty come to me for counseling, and who were both willing to employ and practice these basic simple principles (which we will set forth later in detail), end their marriage with a divorce. For the same valid reasons, for more than 30 years, I have made a standing rule that under no circumstances will I perform a wedding without pre-marital counseling. The bride and groom are required to be counseled together, never separately. In the first 20 years of my ministry, for lack of an understanding of marriage, and to accede to the request and seeming convenience of a couple, I have allowed myself to be aroused out of sleep at 2:00 a.m., and even awaken my wife to be a legal witness, or even get in my car and drive 10 to 20 miles to the county line, when the licenses were issued in an adjoining county, to perform a legal marriage. May God forgive and heal the damage I did in those years through my ignorance, but dedication to serve my fellow man.

I only know of two couples, at this date, of the many couples that I have married in the more than 30 years, after giving them pre-marital counseling, whose marriages have ended in the divorce courts. There could, of course, be some about which I do not know, for I have performed marriages in many states, nations, continents, and even one on the "high seas." Of the two marriages that I know ended in a broken home, one was an uncontested divorce and the mother got custody of their two-year-old child. The other, a legal separation, was a long bitter court fight for the custody of their one child. These breaches of family relations should never have happened in either family. I performed the two marriages after I had officially retired. Feeling I knew these people and their families so well, and that they really understood and knew what marriage was, I had a very brief pre-marital session with each couple on the day of their wedding, which I now realize was a serious error.

Not only do I have confidence in and fully believe what I tell each couple, but I have found the material to be an effective interpretation, philosophy, and workable explanation of marriage.

For more than 30 years, when a couple comes to me with a marital problem, I have consistently asked one question of them, "Did you have pre-marital counseling by a minister, counselor, doctor, or anyone else in the professional field? Did you have pre-marital counseling at all?" The answer has been unanimously, 100%, "No, Chaplain, we did not."

Nonetheless, pre-marital counseling, as poor and lame as it may have been, must be of some effect, or it seems to me that out of the hundreds of cases, sometimes a half dozen cases in one day, in all these years I would have had just one couple who had been counseled, but had not listened to the pre-marital counselor; but I have not had a single case, to date, except the two marriages that I lost, in my retirement years, by my brief and inadequate counseling, and I did not have to ask them, I knew the answer.

As in pre-marital counseling, when a married couple is having marital difficulties I require both husband and wife to be present for at least the initial session of counseling. I do not have any real difficulty in getting both to come together because I can fully assure them that neither of them will be embarrassed. I will not talk to either of them alone. I will not let either of them, alone or together, tell me anything about their difficulty before I talk to them in the initial interview session. In fact, I will do 99.9% of the talking in the first interview session. I only ask them to listen as I tell them about the basic principles that I know they are violating and how these violations are affecting them and their home.

I describe their feelings, knock a lot of their mudholes dry, and plow through some of their precious china closets like the proverbial bull. You see, they both know I do not personally know anything at all about their personal family problems and difficulties and their marital behavior because I have refused to let either of them tell me anything except to say, "Chaplain, we are having family or marital troubles"; that is as far as I let either of them go when I am first contacted for counseling. Sometimes it takes a telephone call to get the other mate in, but they always come after I assure them that they will not be embarrassed. The belligerent mate always warms up soon after the interview gets underway.

Since all disruptions of a marriage are basically for the same reasons, that is, the violation of certain basic principles of behavior, I can relate the larger percentage of their problems and their behaviors and reactions to them. I know they are violating certain principles or they would not be there for help. Thus, I can give them information, insight, understanding and confidence in their own ability to solve their problems. This also gives them confidence in the chaplain as a counselor, because they feel he knows what he is talking about since he has so accurately and vividly described and outlined their difficulties. He has given them the tool and know-how with which to work. They have not been embarrassed by having to tell him any of the details, nor are there any charges or counter-charges — in fact, they have told the counselor nothing. But they now know what is wrong and why, and how to solve it. They know neither is wholly blameless, but each had contributed to the difficulty and both had been the creators of their situation and problems. The only thing with which they are now faced is their own personal integrity and willingness to face each other and solve their own problems.

We must recognize that the success of this relationship — this unique adventure in life — is dependent wholly upon you and your mate. Your marriage cannot be run, dictated, formalized, dominated, ordered, or created by any other person or any other outside force. These other people include the mother-in-law, father-in-law, brothers, sisters, head of the family tribe, etc. These other outside forces include customs, social standing, prestige, traditions, social pressures, fads, popular opinions, etc. Your marriage cannot be controlled by economic or political factors. No force outside you and your mate can control your marriage (unless YOU allow such control).

Ninety-eight percent of these cases do not need to come back for even a second session, even though they are always invited to come back (and I stress this, leaving the way wide open), together or separately. I will see either or both of them at any time after the first session, but seldom do they need to come back. I have often seen them in the worship services the next Sunday, or at a filling station, or Post Exchange, or a bowling alley, or maybe through a call over the telephone or by seeing the husband at his office or place of work and they will say, "Thank you, Chaplain, we got it all worked out," or "We are doing better," or "I think Jim and I will make it now," etc. However, it is true that I do not hear from all of them. (Often the original counseling took place in a foreign land.) But sometimes, years later, I may look down from the pulpit and there they sit, with from one to five children they did not have when I last counseled them. As they leave the chapel or the church, they give a warm greeting, "Well, you see we made it OK," and then introduce the new members of the family — their children.

Chapter Five
That Memorable Day

In brief, here are some of my basic findings and proven theories. For 20 years, I lived with "that woman" (who is still my wife of over 55 years) whom I had married. I tried to understand her reaction and behavior toward me. I tried to give and be forgiving; I thought I was going more than half way. Even though she did not act or react like any other woman I had ever known (she is the only wife I ever had), I was forced to the conclusion that it was just her. She did things that way because she wanted to, arbitrarily — it was just the way "that woman" did things.

I knew she (the only woman in the world able to do so) could and did leave me standing in the middle of the floor feeling as if my feet were nailed down, my hands were tied to my sides, my mouth was sealed, and a little blue blaze was coming out of the top of my head. I knew she was the ONLY woman in the world who did, and could, affect me like that, but "that woman" could and did. I did not know why; in fact, I had not even asked myself the question, "Why?"

Nonetheless, the question, "Why?" became a living reality, one Saturday, when I horrifyingly discovered what I surely did not know about myself, as a husband, that I was "that man." It was a nice, warm, spring-like Saturday noon with the sun shining brightly. I was the Base Chaplain of an Air Force Base in Texas. We were working five and one half days. We lived two miles from the main gate of the Base. All the other Chaplains and Chaplain's Assistants had gone to lunch. Eleven-thirty was the beginning of lunch time. I was about to close the office to go home for lunch when the local florist came in with the fresh cut flowers for the chapel altar. We got fresh flowers each week for Sunday services. Being the only one there, I received the flowers and proceeded to arrange them in two vases on the altar. I saw some of the flowers in the old bouquets were still beautiful and crisp, so from the two vases, I salvaged a very nice bouquet. I wrapped the flowers in a newspaper and let it fan out at the top in a funnel shape. I picked up my briefcase, locked the office, and headed to the car and for home.

We had a circle driveway in our backyard, so I stopped the car at the door of our screened-in back porch. The porch was three steps above the driveway. With the flowers in my left arm and my briefcase in my right hand, I was having a little trouble opening the screen door. Bonnie Ruth, my wife, was in the kitchen. I guess she heard the car stop and looked out of the kitchen door, which was in line with the porch screen door. In that athletic, energetic manner of hers, she sprang out the kitchen door and pushed open the screen door. I was down two steps below and she could look down in the newspaper in my arm and see the flowers. I saw her peeping over to see the flowers and said, "Oh, these are some flowers I brought; I thought you might be able to use them somewhere in the house." She bent over and took the flowers from my arm and said, "Flowers for me, you brought me some flowers." She burst into tears with a loud boo-hoo, whirled around, and ran into the kitchen. I hastily followed and said, "Wait a minute, woman, I did not buy these flowers. They're just some I salvaged from the old bouquet on the chapel altar when I replaced them with fresh flowers a while ago."

Tears still flowing, and holding the newspaper with the flowers in her arm close to herself, she replied, "I don't care if they did come from the altar flowers; you brought me some flowers. We have been married 20 years and you have never brought me any flowers before."

True or not; I really do not know, whether this was the first time I had ever brought any flowers home. I do not remember the details and exact sequence of things for the rest of that day. I was overwhelmed and stunned. What became of the flowers, whether we had lunch, where the children were, I do not know. Maybe Bonnie Ruth knows and remembers — I have never asked her — but all I know was that the flower incident freed the way for our communication and we were able to express our real selves and feelings as we had never, in 20 years, been able to do. I only remember Bonnie Ruth and myself setting at our empty kitchen table, talking to each other in a frank, free, and unreserved manner of conversation as we had never done before. There was no argument, no anger, just baring our feelings and our innermost souls. All of what we talked about and said I do not remember, but the deep driving emotion and feeling of compassion made of a mixture of love and frustration, out of which we were able to bare our souls, empty ourselves, and tenderly express our feelings toward each other, I do remember.

I told her that I could not understand the way she acted. I told her how she affected me the way no other woman in the world did. In fact, she was just "that woman" — I believed she acted the way she did just because she chose to do things that way. At this point — just out of the blue sky — this illustration came to me to explain to her how she affected me. I said, "You leave me standing in the middle of the room, as if my feet were nailed to the floor, my hands were tied at my sides, my mouth was taped shut, and a little blue blaze was coming out of the top of my head." These were such strange words to me, but they said it all for me. She perfectly understood them, too. They said for her exactly the way she felt, too. Because, to my utter amazement, she straightened up in her chair, her eyes widened a little through her tears, a sparkle came in her eyes with a knowing and understanding expression of what I had said, and she said, "That is exactly the way you affect me."

Our marriage, lives, and relationship have never been the same since that memorable Saturday noon, some 35 years ago. Because that Saturday I was astonished and shocked to learn that I — that understanding, giving, forgiving, tolerant man, trying hard to be a good husband to "that woman" — was indeed "that man" to that beloved woman whom I had always introduced as "my wife," yes, my prized possession. I, the man who was trying to be a perfect husband, was "that man"? I affected her the way she affected me; leaving her standing in the middle of the floor, feet nailed to it, her hands tied to her sides, her mouth taped shut, and a blue blaze emitting from her head? This just could not be so; but it was a reality. She firmly and solemnly said so.

What a shock and what a revelation! Her declaration opened for me an entirely new and different viewpoint, angle of vision, and consideration (as well as a multitude of unanswered questions) concerning the marriage relationship between a husband and his wife and vice-versa. Now, I am, in my stunned emotions, setting there looking at "that woman," with tears streaming down her face and a voice as soft and compassionate as an angel, say, "For 20 years, you have affected me in the same way as your illustration describes me as affecting you. I have tried so hard to do things right, please and get along with you, but I could not find the way to do so."

But why and how? I knew, for 20 years, I had been trying sincerely and honestly to be a good, reasonable, considerate, and faithful husband to "that woman," who seemed to do so many things just arbitrarily and without rhyme or reason. I could not make her see or do things differently concerning the family situation or circumstance. I simply could not handle her like I had before we were married or like I handled other women. Now I realized that she, also, had been trying to put things together to understand my reaction and behavior. There had to be some reason for our feelings and lack of understanding of each other for our lives to be at the point they had reached. There had to be an answer. But what was it? What could we do about it?

I had to know the answer. What I thought was unique to me had happened to both of us. When something happens one time only, we think of it as a unique, freak, accidental, etc. and the happening does not offer much, if any, encouragement to be researched as to its origins. I was not a very good scientist, but had learned that anything having happened more than one time was researchable. Here was "this thing" — it had been and was happening to two people; hence, it was researchable. That was not much to start on, but it was too much to ignore; here, I found a place for research to begin. What was the basis or meaning or significance or relationship of this shared helpless feeling in our marriage? Surely it must be related in some way to my wife's and my "marital relationship," but how? Was "this thing" happening to other married couples? I had to know.

Chapter Six
The Research Begins

Did this "phenomenon experience" happen this way to other married couples? How did they affect and understand the reactions of each other? At this time, there were three couples who came to mind. Within a few days, I had carefully approached these couples (John and Susan, Tom and Mary, Jim and Emma — not their real names) whom Bonnie Ruth and I knew rather well, as they often visited in our home and we visited in theirs, our children played together, etc. I decided to begin my research with these six people. It took several weeks because I did not want any one of them to know I had asked the other wife or husband about his or her marital relationship.

Jim was the oldest and really the leader of the group. I managed to get him alone one day out at the air base. "Jim," I said, "I would like to talk to you about Bonnie Ruth." He said certainly. I continued, "Jim, I love Bonnie Ruth very much. But 'that woman' can, at times, do and say things that will, in effect, leave me standing in the middle of the room with the feeling that my feet are nailed to the floor, my hands are tied to my sides, my mouth is taped shut, and a little blue blaze is coming out of the top of my head. But I don't suppose Mary (his wife) ever affects you like that?" Jim's eyes opened a bit wider and he looked straight into my eyes when he said, "Oh, but she does!" Before he had time to question me, I said, "Thank you, Jim," and turned and walked away. A few days later, I was also able to see Emma, Jim's wife. I asked Emma if I could talk with her for a moment, confidentially. She looked a little puzzled, but said of course. I gave her the same illustration as above on how my wife affected me, and then added, "I don't suppose Jim affects you like that." Emma's facial expression brightened up with that womanly intuitive understanding and knowing, and said, "Oh, yes, he surely does!" Then, without giving her time to say any more, I said, "Thank you, Emma," and quickly walked away.

Over the next few weeks, I managed to see each of the other two couples. I asked them the same question, using the same illustration (always privately and confidentially). From each of them I got the same positive response, "Oh, but she does!" and "He surely does!" etc.

Now this experience was no longer confined to Bonnie Ruth and me, but had, by careful and valid research, been expanded to include eight individual experiences in this marital relationship. Was this "phenomenon experience," as I called it then, something actually experienced by all married couples? Was this "phenomenon experience" common to or an inherent element in the marital relationship — was it a common element in all marriages? Why and how does this happen? Why and how could a husband or wife affect the other in this way? Something was basically wrong, but what was it? All I absolutely knew then was that Bonnie Ruth, my wife, could maddeningly, distressfully, and furiously affect me as no other woman in the whole wide world ever had or could. But she could and did. Why and how she affected me this way, I did not know, but I had to find the answer.

Only about six weeks had passed since that memorable Saturday when I had given Bonnie Ruth

The Research Begins

that handful of flowers, gotten from the discarded chapel altar flowers, that had started all this marital relationship revelation and the little research I had done with three other couples. Nonetheless, the "must know" and "had to know" desire for the answer to this newly discovered "phenomenon experience" had now become an obsession with me — a deep burning in my very bones and in the very depth of my soul. Little did I realize then that it would be weeks, months, and years of hard work and through many hundreds of long weary hours of marital counseling that, little by little and bit by bit, I would come to learn the answer.

Just when (day and hour) I came into the knowledge of the answer to why my wife could and did affect me as no other women in the whole world could I will never know. I only know I came to realize the answer. And for many, many years, now, my wife can no longer affect me as if I was standing in the middle of the room with my feet nailed to the floor, my hands tied to my sides, my mouth taped closed, and a little blue blaze coming out of the top of my head. Nor can I, her husband, any longer affect her that way because we both now know better. We both know what we were doing wrong in our marital relationship during the first 20 years of our 55 years of married life. Thanks to God and a handful of salvaged flowers given to Bonnie Ruth one Saturday some 35 years ago for starting us on the right road.

Now, if it happens to eight of us, how about others, so my research began in earnest. My search went on through every state in the Union, including the two new states when they were still territories, and on into Europe, the Near East, the Far East, and Africa; into some 38 nations, islands, and four continents over a period of several years. The answer has been the same from American Indian, Canadian, Mexican, Russian, Scandinavian, Balkan, German, French, Irish, Scottish, English, Italian, Arabian, Jewish, Japanese, Korean, Chinese, Panamanian, Puerto Rican, Filipino, etc. (to name a few) nationalities, cultures, and home lives studied — "she or he does affect me like that" was always the answer from each of them when I would describe my feelings by the illustration given to them as stated above.

How such a simple and insignificant act (giving some flowers) could trigger the unknown, release the emotions, immediately open the way for unrestrained and meaningful communication, set in motion, and determine the direction of events was surely none other than Divine guidance. This act was destined to change drastically my marital relationship and my understanding of marriage. Now I, as a minister and marital counselor, made pre-marital counseling an absolute requirement before I would perform the marriage ceremony. Also, I would use the same method and instruction that I used for pre-marital counseling effectively to keep a marriage in trouble from breaking up and heading for divorce. This is nothing short of a miracle.

Why is it that whether you have been married to "that woman" or "that man" for three days or thirty years, you still do not know how to handle that person and know what to do with her or him? "That man" or "that woman" does not act or react like any other man or woman you have ever known. Surely, that person acts the way he or she does just arbitrarily.

Now, my dear friend, I know from personal experience that you are experiencing all that I have described above, UNLESS you know what marriage really is; unless you know the marriage relationship is unique to all other relationships experienced between human beings. If you are not aware the marriage relationship is a unique relationship between you and your spouse, then "that woman" or "that man" you married (whether one or ten different marriages) can, and does, at times, affect you as if you were standing in the middle of the room, your feet were nailed to the floor, your hands were tied to your side, your mouth was sealed shut, and a little blue blaze was coming out of the top of your head.

My understanding of marriage and the marital relationship before that memorable Saturday event was next to nothing — just about zero. I did not know what a "wife" was. I did not know she could not act like my mother, my sister, or any other women on earth — she could not even act like she did when she was my girl friend — because she was none of these; she was my wife. Therefore, she could only act and react toward me as a wife, the position or status that she, of her own free will, had assumed when she, too, had answered "I do" to the question posed by the minister, "Do you take this man to be your lawful husband," etc. in our wedding ceremony.

Regardless of what either of us knew or understood about the marriage relationship, she had assumed the unique status of "my wife" and I had assumed the unique status of "her husband." Whether she or I knew or understood this did not change the fact that she could now only act in the role of a "wife" to me and could not act as my mother, sister, girl friend, or female acquaintance because she was none of those. She was my wife and could only act in our marital relationship in this newly acquired and unique role, and in no other way.

The legal grounds for divorce have not occupied much of my time and thought. I have left that area to the lawyers, theologians, and sociologists to wrestle with and give expert answers. What has commanded my time and deep concern is how, and in what way, a man and a woman can be joined in marriage so the "two become one," thereby making divorce impossible, because they are one — inseparable. For "from the beginning" of marriage — from the first man and woman — the Creator intended that "the two shall become one;" therefore, "from the beginning," divorce was nonexistent.

Chapter Seven
Defense Mechanisms

I do not remember the exact day or hour when I came to find a fully satisfactory answer for myself as to why Bonnie Ruth could affect me as she could and did. I suppose it came gradually, over a period of time, as I learned and worked it out in my sincere and honest struggles in trying to help others find the answer when they came to me for counsel with their marital problems. Somehow, though, I discovered the answer was related to our basic personal "defense mechanisms". I found that every human being, regardless of sex, race, language, culture, nationality, education, and social standing uses these same basic "defense mechanisms" from infancy to the grave. I discovered there were two, and only two, "defense mechanisms" known to man or beast and they were universally employed in the everyday living of each and every human being, as well as the insects, birds, fish, and all the animals. These basic "defense mechanisms" did work successfully, to a more or less degree, on every other human being in every walk of life from king to peasant, emperor to subject, president to waterboy, with only one exception — the husband and wife relationship.

Now I knew the answer to why Bonnie Ruth could create in me (and I in her) the feeling of my feet nailed to the floor, my hands tied to my sides, my mouth sealed shut, with only an angry emitting feeling, silently boiling within me. She can no more create in me (nor I in her) this angry, helpless feeling (from which too many marriages break out into violence —

wife beating, stabbing or shooting a husband or wife to death (see Chapter Ten) because we both now know that feeling's source and how we have to handle the situations that arise. Now we know why, in those first 20 years of marriage, we could at various times create a silent and motionless hell within each other: it was because we were still trying to be decent and respectable human beings, but trying to use our old "defense mechanisms," that we had used to try to solve all our problems from the cradle to the grave, and to try to deal with or handle our marriage relationship, which will not work in the marital relationship to any degree. I will discuss this more in detail later.

This "silent, motionless hell" was created for me because I could not get my ideas, opinions, and wishes across. In other words, I could not demand my will and have my own way by the use of the "defense mechanism" of force (which some authorities call the "fight defense mechanism"). Even books have been written on "how to fight fair" in marriage. Many scholars have taught that ministers and counselors should develop techniques to help husbands and wives learn how to "fight." This is absolutely wrong. Conflict in marriage is neither necessary nor desirable. The theory of conflict in marriage held by these scholars is not only unnecessary, undesirable, dangerous, degrading, undignified, and non-creative, it is also incompatible with the teachings of God (as were laid out previously in Chapter Two). This is the one unique relationship where conflict cannot work and need never arise. The "defense mechanisms" can never be used in the marital relationship and, therefore, conflict can never occur if they are never used.

When a difference arose between us, and was not amiably resolved, then anger arose. My impulse would be to employ the force "defense mechanism" and just kick my wife out and through the door. But, trying to be a decent, respectable husband (besides it being against my culture and training and against the law in many geographic locations to kick your wife out and through the door), my foot had to stay on the floor as if it was nailed there. That feeling only intensified my emotions because I was denied the physical actualization of kicking her out and through the door. I might have the urge to plant my fist in her eye or on the end of her nose, but for the same reasons of decency and self-restraint, I did not move my arm and hand. Thus, my hands were useless as if tied to my sides. My pent-up anger might tempt me to try to beat her down with words, to tell her what and how I was thinking and feeling — which would not be very complimentary — and verbally to cut her down, verbally reducing her to shreds. (In marital counseling, I would much rather deal with a literal black eye or bloody nose than a badly verbally shredded case. The physical wounds heal much sooner and better and leave fewer scars.) Nonetheless, for the same reason my foot and hand were motionless, my tongue must remain silent and my mouth closed — the only thing left then being the "blue blaze" of emotion boiling within my mind and nervous system. But, thank God, Bonnie Ruth and I cannot affect each other like that any more, since we now know better, and also know why our normal "defense mechanisms" cannot be used on each other, because we are married — husband and wife.

The moment a couple, within a wedding ceremony, says, "I do," these two "defense mechanisms" go out the door of their marriage relationship — whether they know it or not, whether they like it or not — it is a fact. The wedding ceremony literally strips the couple naked of the "defense mechanisms." If the two are to "become one," as Jesus said marriage was intended by the Creator in the beginning (Mark 10:6-8), the "defense mechanisms" can never be used in their marriage relationship. In fact, the "defense mechanisms" cannot be used at all, because the marital relationship cannot to any degree respond to "avoidance" and "force." Trying to employ the "defense mechanisms" in marriage only creates a "living hell" rather than a "loving home" for the marriage.

DEFENSE MECHANISM
1. Definition
2. Only Two

Perhaps I should explain what I mean by "defense mechanism." I am using the words in the same sense and meaning as *Webster's Dictionary* defines them:

> DEFENSE: (1) Resistance to or protection from attack. (2) A means of warding off attack or danger.

> MECHANISM: (1) The parts of a machine, taken collectively; the arrangement or relation of the parts of anything as adapted to produce an effect. (2) Mechanical operation or action.

Now, when we put the two words together, we are still using them in the same general sense and definition as the dictionary:

DEFENSE MECHANISM: (1) A defensive reaction by an organism, as against disease germ. (2) A mode of behavior, or a belief, adopted by a person to conceal the true condition pertaining to himself or his beliefs. (3) The combination of mental processes by which a result is obtained, as the mechanics of invention.

When the dictionary puts the two words together, "defense mechanism," the dictionary definition of the combination almost, but not quite, gives us our full definition. The dictionary writers seem not to have conceived of the idea that by "defense mechanism," we also try to keep situations and people out of our lives, try not to become involved in anything we do not like or wish to be a part of, nor to have it relate to us. I feel this is an important element missing in the dictionary definition. I believe a simple illustration of what I mean by "defense mechanism" can easily be understood.

Suppose you are walking along the street with your wife. Suddenly, out of the neighbor's yard rushes an angry dog about to attack your wife, who is the one nearest the yard. You grab a nearby stick of wood and stop the dog's attack while your wife runs down the street out of range of the dog, for it is on a long leash tethered too near the street. Thus, you continue to keep the dog at bay with the stick of wood while you slowly back away. This is what I mean by defense. You defended your wife and yourself from the attack and possible harm by a vicious or angry dog. The stick of wood was the mechanical device, or mechanism, or object that you used to ward off the attack of the vicious and angry dog. A "defense mechanism" is the means, instrument, object, or mechanism used to defend ourselves against anything that we do not like and to keep any thing, event, situation, or person out of our lives — anything we do not want in our lives or to become a part of our lives.

What are these two "defense mechanisms" used universally by all of us from the cradle to the grave? They can be called avoidance and force, or flight and fight as applied to the history of men and nations, or to the fish, fowl, and animal kingdoms. Basically, no other "defense mechanisms" are known to or used by the human race. In the previous illustration, the husband used force to beat off the dog, while the wife used avoidance by running down the street to get out of reach of the dog.

We always try to avoid anything that we do not like. "If you don't play dolls like I want to play dolls, I'll take my dolls and go home," or "If you don't play marbles like I want to play marbles, I'll pick up my marbles and put them in my pocket." The Psalmist employed this "defense mechanism" on the wicked and on his enemies.

But, if we cannot avoid the situation by running away, then if some other fact, element, circumstance, or motive prompts, we have, "I am larger and stronger than you are, so if you don't play dolls like I want to play dolls, I'll slap your jaws and pull your hair. Or if you don't play marbles like I play marbles, I will black your eye and kick you in the pants until you acknowledge that 'liners is out,' or the 'taw line' is here and not there."

What in the world has all this to do with the basic principles of marriage, and what is so unique about "avoidance" and "force," because we have been using them all our lives? Simply this: Yes, you have used them all your life on everybody you have met, but the relationship between a wife and husband is an EXCEPTION — "defense mechanisms" cannot be successfully used to any degree in marriage, either by a husband on his wife or by a wife on her husband and still have a home. If you try to use avoidance, you have nothing. You cannot take your dolls and go to Mama and have a home of your own. You cannot walk out and slam the door behind your and head into the wide open road or some other place and have your home. No, avoidance cannot be used and still have a home. If you try to use force, you do not have a home, you have turmoil in which to live; often a veritable living hell, not a loving home.

Chapter Eight
Relationships

Before we go further in this phase, let us examine another aspect seeming to be overlooked by counselors, ministers, and psychologists with reference to the "marriage relationships" to other "human relationships." Perhaps the diagram below will help explain what I am trying to convey.

Take a sheet of paper, put a black dot in the center of the page, about ¾ of the way down from the top, and under this dot write the word "me." (I do this whether working in pre-marital or marital counseling. The dot becomes personalized and can be used to counsel 1 or 100 people simultaneously with the same effect.) From this dot, draw a series of vertical straight lines in a fan shape. Normally, I use eight lines, but I only draw two lines to begin with and add the others, two at a time, as we explain, analyze, and understand what each line represents. When I come to the last two lines, they are always drawn straight out (at 90° angles) to the right and left of the dot. This actually forms a straight line with the dot in the middle.

●
ME

Let the first two fan lines represent your mother and father.

```
F   M
 \ /
  ●
  ME
```

I know this much about you — biologically, I know you had a mother and a father or you would not be here. Hence, you should personally know the father and mother relationship. However, because of death or divorce, this knowledge may have been dimmed or may even be non-existent. But even with a foster parent, you learned not to expect your father to act or react to a situation involving you in exactly the same way as your mother would or did act or react. Your mother's and the father's reactions to your situation are related, but definitely different, human reactions. Nonetheless, you grow up expecting these different reactions and they become parts of your everyday life.

The next two lines on the fan represent brother and sister relationships.

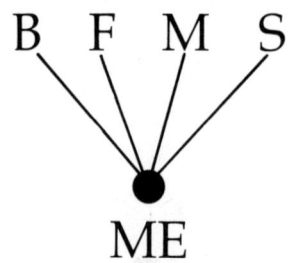

```
B   F   M   S
 \  \ /  /
    ●
    ME
```

I do not have a brother, so I have never personally experienced that brother-to-brother family relationship.

I have to rely on the experience of others as they may relate it to me. However, I do have three sisters. I know by experience what that relationship is. I have found by experience that my sisters did not act or react to a situation involving me in the same way my mother did, yet their reactions were related. They were female. They were blood kin. We lived in the same house, under the same comfort or hardship. But the fact was, I grew up understanding and expecting my sisters each to react differently to a given situation involving me, and most assuredly not like my mother. We can see and, hopefully, agree that I would not expect a brother to react like my father, although their actions and reactions are related. Each is an accepted, different, acknowledged, and understood human relationship to me and my situation. This explanation of father, mother, brother, sister reactions is not out of the ordinary and not difficult to understand. In your own experiences, you have learned to expect and accept these different reactions to the same incident by different members of your family.

The next two lines represent the boy friend and girl friend relationships.

BF   B   F   M   S   GF

●
ME

Here we are on mutual ground because I know you have had experience in this relationship — if this is premarital counseling, this is your present status; if you are married, this was your previous status. Again, we apply the principles that we have discussed to this known and acknowledged relationship. We agree that a woman would not expect her boy friend to act or react to her in a given situation as would her father or her brother. Neither would a man expect his girl friend to act or react like his mother or sister. These different human relationships can be carried farther to the casual friend, complete stranger, etc. However, I believe that by this time, I have gotten the point across that you know more than one human relationship and you expect different reactions to a given situation from each and every one of these people, even though they may be closely related or total strangers, they are definitely recognizable and identifiable human experiences and relationships. You have tried to handle, solve, or deal with all of these relationships through the use of the two "defense mechanisms" of avoidance and force.

Now we come to the straight horizontal lines.

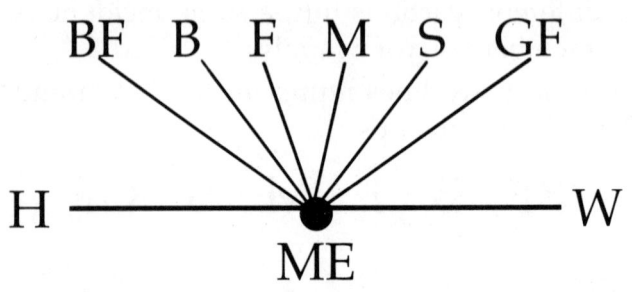

```
      BF  B  F  M  S  GF
        \  \  \ | /  /
         \  \  \|/  /
H ─────────●───────── W
           ME
```

These represent the husband and wife. Here are two new relationships, but as real as the father, mother, brother, sister, boy friend, and girl friend relationships. This relationship must be recognized as a new human relationship because it must be handled differently from all our other human relationships. On our diagram, these two people do not belong among the upright lines of our illustration because they are unique, which I will explain later.

Why are the actions of this woman or this man represented on the horizontal line so confusing to you? Why does she or he not react like any other man or woman you have ever known? Now, you are beginning to recognize your spouse is not your mother, nor your sister, nor your father, nor your brother, nor is that person still your girl friend or boy friend; therefore, that person should not act or react like any or all of them — that person is your "wife" or "husband." She or he must be, and is, acting in that capacity, in this new and strange role for both of you.

Marriage is not only a new human relationship created in your life, but marriage is a unique relationship — there is no other human relationship like it. Not all your confusion has been cleared up just to know you are a husband or a wife and react only as a husband or a wife and do not respond like any of the other known relationships of which you have knowledge. Although you may now understand your spouse does act and react differently than other person you have known because your spouse is acting and reacting as your husband or wife, you are still asking why and how your spouse affects you as he or she does (the nailed feet, tied hands, sealed mouth, and blue blaze idea). That is the way you may and can make each other feel. But why can you not make each other understand and why will you both not seem to do things right? You cannot "make" each other do anything. But the question is, "Why?" You could handle your father and brother, and mother and sister, and even your boy friend or girl friend, when you were dating, before you were married, to a more or less successful degree, but why is your wife or husband so — "well, so stubborn."

Chapter Nine
Defense Mechanisms
In Relationships

To begin to help you understand the answers to these questions, I must now help you recognize the use of the two "defense mechanisms" that you have used all your lives and how the "defense mechanisms" cannot be used in your marriage relationship. All your lives you have tried to avoid things that you did not like or did not wish to be a part of your lives.

As a girl, do not tell me when you got angry with your daddy, you did not leave the room, go to your bedroom, and shut the door behind you; or you went out of the house for a walk — you put distance between your dad and yourself. Do not tell me you have never been playing out back of the house, or the other side of the barn, or over in the neighbor's yard and your mother called; you heard her, but you ignored the call and acted as if you did not hear her. Also, when you were playing dolls with a neighbor girl and she would not or did not play dolls like you wanted to, then you gathered up your dolls and went home. Maybe you were playing dolls with a sister, she was not playing like you wanted to, they were your dolls, so you gathered them up, put them away, and went to play elsewhere. What are you doing here — "avoiding" the situation, running away from what and whom you do not like at the moment. All your life, you used this avoidance mechanism on your father, mother, brother, sister, playmates at school, and even your school teachers, but you cannot use it on Tom (or Melvin or James) since you are married and have a home.

Now to use the same situations again.

Defense Mechanisms:
1 Avoidance
2. Force

You are angry at your father, but you burst into tears and play on his emotions, get his sympathy, and he feels guilty with a hurt look; he even tries to grant a few extra concessions to you. You may be angry at your mother; you may pout, sulk, slam things around as you wash dishes or clean house. Perhaps the neighbor girl or your sister with the dolls, when they do not play like you want them to play, you slap their jaws and pull their hair. You have handled each of these situations differently, but this time you used force to get your way. This is employing the other "defense mechanism" — force.

Young man, you have been using that force "defense mechanism" since you were three days old. You learned the wider you opened your mouth and the louder you cried, the quicker someone came to your crib and attended your desires or needs. It may be that you were really defending yourself against an empty stomach (you were hungry), or an open safety pin was sticking you, or a soiled diaper needed changing. Nevertheless, you soon learned, though, that none of these were needed. When you hollered loud and long, someone would come to pick you up, cuddle and love you, and you liked that very much.

Love is important. In fact, love is absolutely essential to the human existence. This fact has been

Defense Mechanisms in Relationships

scientifically proven by experiments in France by a French scientist and by similar experiments performed by Erick Erickson, here in America, with infant babies. The babies were given the best care known to science — the best food, clothing, and medical care — everything except recognition and love. They were cared for and handled like delicate or fragile objects, but no responses of recognition or affection or love were given. That is, the babies were never permitted to be cuddled and loved. Results — all the French babies died before they were three years old. All the Erickson babies dwindled and died before they were nine months old, for no apparent cause or reason. The conclusion was that human beings cannot live or survive without love or without personal recognition, as the French called it.

Meanwhile, back at the baby bed, you had by force — loud crying — caused your mother to pick you up, cuddle and love you, and you liked that. But you did not stop there in your baby bed. You have been using that "defense mechanism" of force, hollering loud and long in varying degrees ever since, on everyone you have met and known — father, mother, brother, sister, schoolmates, teachers, girl friends — to a more or less successful degree, depending on the situation and the person. You had your effect on each of them. You are still trying to use the same "defense mechanism" on your wife, but it has not, will not, in fact cannot, work on her because she is your wife. The marriage relationship is unique and cannot respond to the "defense mechanisms," the only two known to man or beast — avoidance and force. You can and have used avoidance and force to varying degrees and with varying success on all humans you have known, but when you said, "I do" in the wedding ceremony, at that moment these "defense mechanisms" went out the door, and can never to any degree be successfully used in the marital relationship, mutually established that day and hour in the marriage vow by the two of you.

Consider the "defense mechanism" of "avoidance."

Defense Mechanisms:
1. Avoidance
"Act of Avoiding; Keeping Clear of"

Young woman, you can use avoidance on me 100% effectively. You can say, "I don't like that old chaplain; I will never go in his office again." You can refuse to open the door or invite me in when I make a pastoral call to your home. You see me coming down the street and you cross over to the other side of the street or go around the corner; hence, you can avoid me 100%. I am then out of your association and life. On the other hand, your husband lives in the same house as you. You cannot avoid him to any degree and still have a home. You cannot pick up your bonnet and go home to Mama and have a home. You cannot refuse to acknowledge your husband's presence in the house, refuse to speak to him (the silent treatment), and still have a home. No, avoidance will not work to any degree on your husband.

When you and your husband were girl friend and boy friend, if you had a little spat or disagreement, you could give him his hat and tell him that it was time to go home; or he could pick up his hat and announce that he was leaving. You would not answer his telephone calls, or he just did not call you all week.

This worked to some degree until you both finally got back on speaking terms. Now that you are married, you cannot give your husband his hat and tell him to leave, or he cannot pick up his hat and walk out, when the two of you have a little spat or disagreement and have a home.

Now, consider the "defense mechanism" of force.

Defense Mechanism

2. Force
  A. Physical
  B. Mental
  C. Moral
  D. Spiritual

If on 2 out of every 3 days when your husband comes in from work, you met him at the door and hit him in the eye or punched him in the nose, physically or verbally — for your own reasons — pretty soon he is going to get shy or apprehensive about coming through that door at all. He will, at least, delay coming home. Your husband might go by the club or bar and have a drink, or stay late at the office, etc. Eventually he will say he has had enough and will not come home at all. However, if you let him get in the house before you start hitting him, actually or verbally, you will not have a home, you will have a place — a "living hell." If the two of you have children, they will become confused, nervous, and emotionally disturbed. Respect, order, and discipline in your home will break down, and overflow into the children's school and neighborhood lives. This can become so severe as to end in a mental hospital or criminal institute of corrections. No, the "defense mechanism" of force cannot be used on your husband and have a home. Also, everything herein said to the wife applies equally to the husband's relationship to her.

Chapter Ten
Cause of Wife and Husband Abuse

Whether wife beating and mate abuse are more prevalent today than ever, or whether the newspapers, radio, and television news media are paying more attention to these situations, is an unanswered question. However, any wife or husband abuse should not and need not be acceptable to our enlightened culture and society, nor, for that matter, for any culture or society among human beings who have created homes through marriage. Why should wife abuse and husband abuse exist or be tolerated at all in any sociological setting? I have not noticed any of the news media advocating or defending the practice of wife and husband abuse, but rather they advocate legislation restraining or helping to stop this unwanted and barbaric practice of violence in the home. Nevertheless, it seems legislation, laws, and penalties are not solving the wife and husband abuse problem in this country. Since this violence is not an acceptable situation in the homes of our society, what can be done, if laws and penalties cannot eliminate or handle the situation?

Since the wife and husband abuse occurs only between married couples, it seems reasonable to look for the solution to this dilemma within the marriage relationship itself, rather than looking for an external cure — legislation, courts, lawyers, fines, jail sentences, or divorces. Let me propose seven premises upon which to build a solution to the hideous problem of wife and husband abuse.

First, we need to recognize that marriage is a unique experience within the overall human experience. In other words, there is no other experience known to the human race like marriage. It is not created by nature, but is instituted by God and brought about by man.

Second, we need to realize that since marriage is a unique human experience, it cannot be handled or dealt with in the same manner as other human experiences or relationships.

Third, we need to recognize that conflict is not inherent in marriage (as some authors, professors, and counselors in the field of marriage and family affairs advocate). In contrast, the very opposite is true — LOVE is inherent in marriage.

Fourth, we need to recognize that since marriage is unique to all other human experiences, it cannot respond to the methods and "defense mechanisms" of avoidance and force (basically used to deal with all other human experiences). Therefore, marriage requires a different method, principle, and set of rules to which the marriage relationship can respond.

Fifth, we need to see that since wife and husband abuse only occur within marriage, and this is because the marriage relationship is unique to all other human experiences, then the real prevention and cure for mate abuse would be in the understanding of what the marriage relationship is and knowledge of the rules to which the marriage relationship can respond. Marriage cannot respond to the normal everyday avoidance and force "defense mechanisms" that we have used from the cradle to today in all of our human experiences.

Sixth, we must realize that if mate abuse is ever to be eliminated (which it most definitely could and should be), we need to begin with prevention, that is, pre-marital instruction, counseling, and training. The couple needs to understand what marriage is. They need to know marriage is unique and cannot respond to avoidance and force "defense mechanisms." Therefore, entirely different methods, principles, and rules must be applied to create a loving home, thereby avoiding a "living hell."

Seventh, we must see that legislation, laws, courts, lawyers, and even divorce cannot be ignored in the wife and husband abuse cases, but that the real solution actually lies in the individuals. Both the husband's and wife's personal knowledge and understanding of marriage and their own personal integrity and willingness to do what they know to be right and just must be brought out.

As I have explained previously, Bonnie Ruth and I were married for 20 years before we came to realize we did not know what marriage really was. We did not know how to live with each other effectively and amiably (especially within ourselves). She was past 21 and I was nearing 25 years old when we got married. We were school teachers, fairly mature, and, fortunately, we both had a fairly good moral and religious training and concept of life. These gave us the ability to respect the personality and individual rights of another human being, but we were trying to handle our marital relationship in the same way as we had been trying to handle all of our other human experiences, but without much satisfaction or success.

I had never considered the use of the avoidance mechanism within our marriage — get a divorce. I guess that I was too much of the mind-set of a minister friend of mine, who gave some lectures on marriage to my troops. When one man asked him if he had ever considered getting a divorce from his wife, his answer was, "Consider a divorce no, never; murder, yes." I never considered the use of the avoidance mechanism of separation or divorce. However, deep within me was anger and feeling sorry for myself. She says that the same was true with her.

Our moral and religious training and concepts did not permit us to react to our anger with physical violence like wife beating or husband abuse, but we both realized (although we had never expressed our feelings on this idea to each other until that memorable Saturday) I could not make Bonnie Ruth do anything that she did not want to do. Thus, when Bonnie Ruth would do or say something offensive, or I did not like, or when she would not do something that I was trying to get her to agree to do, the old "defense mechanism" of force would angrily rush into my mind. I would want to kick her physically out the door, or to plant my fist in her eye or on her nose, or at least tell her off with words that would literally cut her to shreds.

However, instead of giving into my emotions and anger, thereby becoming a wife beater, I felt utterly helpless and immobile. Why? Because I was trying to be a good, loving, and decent husband; my personal integrity, moral concept, and respect for the right of another human being; my reputation in the community; and in most states it was against the law to kick your wife out the door or knock her through a window. If I yelled too loudly at her and used improper language, the neighbors would hear me and my social standing and influence as a minister in the community would be damaged. Hence, all that I could do was stand there with my face red, eyes flashing, and a little blue blaze coming out of the top of my head. I was refusing to let my feet, hands, and tongue give vent to my angry emotions and feelings in the form of wife beating, or at least a fight, because she was pretty hefty (she was an athletic coach of basketball, baseball, etc.)

All this was because I did not know why she, when no other women could, affected me as she could and did, and because I did not know marrige was a unique relationship in human experiences; she was my wife and my relationship to her was different from my relationship to any other women in this world — relative or acquaintance — that I had ever met in my life. I did not know this unique relationship (marriage) required a different way, method, principle, and set of rules for dealing with "that woman" to whom I was married — my wife. Nor did she know how to deal with "that man" — her husband. Now, however, for nearly 35 years since we learned the answer to the above mentioned lack of knowledge, we cannot affect each other as we did for the first 20 years of our marriage. Hence, anger and the thought of mate abuse never occupy our thoughts and emotions.

That is really what this book is all about. The marriage relationship is a unique human experience; but it is not mysterious. It can be explained and understood. Marriage cannot respond to the two "defense mechanisms" of avoidance and force (the only two known to man) as means of survival and living; therefore, marriage requires a different method and set of rules to create a "loving home," not a "living hell."

I am sure, because of human nature itself, fear, shame, disregard for laws, disregard for rights of other human beings, etc., the real and ultimate solution to the problem of wife beating and mate abuse does not lie in legislation or laws to eliminate and stop it. I do not, on the other hand, advocate that legislation, courts, lawyers, fines, and jail sentences be abolished or ignored. I am certain the inherent and ultimate solution for eliminating this abominable act of mate abuse lies within prevention. Since wife beating and husband beating can occur only within the marriage relationship, then the preventive measure, or cure, must come from within the realm of the marriage relationship itself.

The first step toward eradicating this dilemma would logically be in pre-marital prevention. The couple, before marriage, should be taught the truth — marriage is unique to all other human experiences — and shown how the marriage relationship cannot respond, in any degree, to avoidance or force. If the couple, before marriage, is taught the simple rule contained in this book that will, when applied to both mates, handle any and every marital relationship trauma that can arise, there would not, in fact could not, be any wife beating or mate abuse or violation of personal dignity and integrity in any given marriage. But what about existing marriages that are in trouble?

The second step toward eliminating this occurrence would be similar to the first. The same information and instructions presented as pre-marital knowledge, for the prevention of the disruption of marriage by mate abuse, are given to a couple whose marriage is in trouble. This same material, if honestly, willingly, and sincerely applied by both the husband and the wife, will absolutely cure spouse abuse. This same knowledge able to create a loving and happy home will hold together a home in the midst of disruption or breaking apart. This information will provide the cure.

There is, however, another phase to this mate abuse problem. Even if the bride and groom to be or the couple already married, with marriage troubles, possessed the needed knowledge to handle effectively and amiably all marriage relationship problems, does each of them possess the moral integrity and self-discipline to apply what they know willingly, honestly, and sincerely? The moral integrity and willingness (and will is basic) to do what one knows is right may be overcome by previously acquired bad habits, bad temper, aggression, guilt, alcohol, drugs, etc. These would need adequate help or counseling and/or medical treatment, or a life-changing religious experience to break the habits and to empty or discharge the subconscious mind of these undesirable materials and habits.

Having spent more than 55 years in this field of counseling human needs, and human nature being what it is, I am much aware there will be, in spite of adequate pre-marital counseling and curative training, other measures of legislative and punitive nature that cannot be eliminated or ignored in our society for the good of the wife, the husband, the children, and the homes of this nation. Nonetheless, I fully believe, based on some 35 years of use in my own marriage and pre-marital and curative counseling to hundreds of couples, that by using the material indicated and taught in this book, the problem of mate abuse can be eliminated to the point where wife beating and husband abuse would become rare incidences — in fact, headline news for all the media on where and when an incidence of abuse occurred.

Chapter Eleven
Marriage Creates
and Takes Away

Whether you wish it that way or not, the unique and inherent power of the wedding ceremony of marriage does strip you of the "defense mechanisms" that you have used all your lives on other people. You can never use the "defense mechanisms" of "avoidance" or "force" on your mate and create a home. By the wedding ceremony, or contract, whether performed by a minister, priest, rabbi, or civil authority, you, the bride and groom, are helplessly stripped of your "defense mechanisms" as literally as if a group of ruffians would meet you at the door after the ceremony and literally strip you of all your clothes and leave you standing there in the nude before friends and spectators. You must fully understand this if you are going to be able to establish a happy and secure home.

If chaplains, priests, rabbis, ministers, and civil authorities only knew and understood this phenomenon — that the marriage ceremony creates a new and unique human relationship that will not, in fact cannot, respond to the normally known and universally used "defense mechanisms" of "avoidance" and "force" — we could remove ourselves from the role of an unwitting ruffian or helpless wretch, standing by and seeing the marriage that we so beautifully created get battered and even broken to pieces by the couple because of our own lack of knowledge and understanding of the marriage relationship. If we only understood this principle, we would always, through pre-marital counseling, explain this unique relationship to the couple considering entering into marriage and give them a set of values or rules that they could substitute for the two "defense mechanisms" of which the marriage ceremony will strip them.

Personally, I strongly feel any official, ecclesiastical, or civil authority performing a marriage ceremony or validating a marriage contract without pre-marital counseling is guilty of ignorant or willful, if not actual, commission of a criminal offense against the couple being married and the society into which this official launches them as man and wife to establish a home. I speak from experience. For 20 years, I was one of these maritally ignorant ministers, who was party to this disastrous situation. And, as a result of this marital ignorance, Bonnie Ruth and I lived together for 20 years as "that woman" and "that man" because we did not know there was any other or better way to live together and to raise our children. Thank God, we did accidentally and gradually learn better and find THE WAY that I am trying to share with you.

In pre-marital conferences, I always stress the idea of you, the couple, discussing and coming to an agreed settlement on all the important and knotty questions, such as religion, children, finances, sex, health, etc., before the wedding. This discussion needs to take place while you still have free use of your two "defense mechanisms" of force and avoidance. If you cannot settle or come to some agreeable understanding about these concepts before the marriage ceremony, while you still have on your "old armor" of "defense mechanisms," you will not be able to settle them after the wedding. After you have been stripped of these "old defense mechanisms," which, whether you know it or not, you definitely will be, you cannot use those mechanisms to work out difficulties again.

In more than 52 years as a counselor in education, ecclesiastical affairs, and life's general situations and problems, experience has taught me that rarely, and only in extraordinary situations, is it wise to give specific and dogmatic advise or formulas to the counselee for the solution to his or her problem. I have found the real answers must come from the individual himself, through my guidance in his thinking and understanding of his situation in order to gain insight into his own problems and to see or realize the answer and solution to his situation.

Hence, I seldom ever give any direct and expecially dogmatic advice or rule of action or behavior to anyone in normal counseling. In counseling on marriage relationships, however, I discovered that an EXCEPTION to the rule needed to be made because the marriage relationship — that is, action and reaction in everyday living between a married couple — will not, in fact cannot, respond to the normally known and used "defense mechanisms" of "avoidance" and "force."

When I discovered this concept, it became very clear to me, out of my own marriage and struggles and out of my experiences of trying to counsel and help other married couples, that a new understanding, set of values, or rules must be found to replace the normally used "defense mechanisms," which the marriage vows had nullified on the wedding day.

This insight did not come through a flash of brilliance, but gradually, by bits and pieces, came out of the struggles of my mind, heart, and soul; aided by others sharing their struggles with me through their marital problems, along with a persistently burning desire and need to know. In fact I was desperate and had to know for myself, sustained by the faith in the belief there really was a logical and knowledgeable answer to a better way of handling and understanding this unique human relationship created by the marriage vows.

Chapter Twelve
The Answer

I believe that I was led by Divine guidance through these struggles (sleepless nights, long working days, weeks, months, years) to a workable solution and answer. Therefore, the answer — this workable and infallible rule — is not mine. It was given to me by Divine guidance through my own marital struggles and the pain, anxieties, heartaches, and disastrous situations of the many married couples who shared with me over these long years of my sincere and diligent search for the truth about this unique human relationship that we call marriage. All the while, if only I had known and understood, the answer had been revealed to the human race and had actually been recorded in written history hundreds, yes thousands, of years ago. "Therefore shall a man leave his father and his mother, and shall cleave unto his wife: and they shall be one flesh" (Genesis 2:24). Many centuries later, the answer was re-stated by Jesus, the only sinless and perfect man to live on this earth, in the following words: "But from the beginning of creation, God made them male and female. For this reason a man shall leave his father and mother and be joined to his wife, and the two shall become one. So they are no longer two, but one" (Mark 10:6-8).

By Divine guidance and through experience and hard work, I have re-stated the principle of this unique human relationship of marriage and expressed it in more current language as an understandable and workable rule — a rule as dependable and infallible as the sun's daily rising in the east and setting in the west. Here it is:

A WILLINGNESS TO SIT DOWN TOGETHER AND, WITH LOVE, TALK OVER ANYTHING AND EVERYTHING, UNEMOTIONALLY.

Brief and simple, yes; but for many years, now, it has worked for Bonnie Ruth and me and it has also worked for all the many couples to whom I have given it in pre-marital counseling, or to whom I have given it for the mending and healing of troubled marriages.

This brief and simple rule is not only infallible when used in the marriage relationship, it is also workable in all person-to-person relationships and in national and international affairs. If presidents, kings, queens, prime ministers, diplomats, commissioners, etc. of all nations were willing to use this single rule, there could never be another war upon this earth. Hence, we would have no need for military might. What a transformation in health and happiness could take place if the world's total military budgets could be effectively applied to food, shelter, and clothing for the people of the earth!

Let us consider this rule and analyze its parts. The first part is a willingness. Both husband and wife have to be willing because neither can make the other do anything. If one person is willing, but the other is not willing, they cannot come to an understanding or agreement. (This is the basic reason why I will not counsel the husband or wife separately in the initial interview. It takes the willing participation of both of them to make this rule operate.)

Your will is the only thing on God's green earth that is yours irrevocably. No man or woman can make me say yes or no, if I do not will to do so. People can apply pressure, tempt, sing beautifully bewitching songs, beat me, and even kill this body and burn it into powder and sift it out to the four winds of the earth, but no human being can make me say or do anything until I am willing. My will has to be broken or become cooperative before I act.

No human being can invade your will and God will not. The Bible says, "Behold I stand at the door and knock; if any man hears my voice, and opens the door, I will come into him, and will eat with him, and he with me" (Revelation 3:20). I could go further and say that God not only will not invade your will and make you do something, but God cannot invade your will and still be your Heavenly Father. He cannot invade your will and make you do anything and still be God — He would be something else. He would then be an intruder, a tyrant, a dictator, or something other than your understanding, loving, Heavenly Father and the God who created you and gave you your will. Now, if neither a human being nor God can invade my life against my will (without my consent), how can you expect a husband and a wife to come to any understanding or agreement without mutual consent (i.e., a willingness of both parts)? This cannot be accomplished; both must be willing.

The second part of the rule is to sit down. This is a psychological gimmick (as I tell counselees) to help create an atmosphere of congeniality. When you are sitting down, your body is not in its normal fighting position. If Tom (or Ray or Carroll) was going to black my eye or bloody my nose, he would not be sitting there so relaxed with his hands laying in his lap or hanging limp at his side. He would be up on his toes, his fists doubled up, ready for the fight. This is the reason I tell people to sit down. Then their bodies are not in a fighting position. Because you have willingly come to your conference, not to fight, but to communicate in love and understanding with each other and come to some mutual decision, sitting down helps overcome and control the old "defense mechanism" of force that you have used on everyone else.

Now, when you sit down, if you say to yourself, "I had better get on my guard and get my best mental armor out here so the old gal (or old boy) can't put anything over on me," then you are doomed for failure because you are using the old defense of avoidance and force — trying to avoid getting trapped, as you put it, and force by outwitting the other. No, you must be willing to sit down (mentally, as well as physically), attentatively listen, and try hard to understand honestly, from word, intimation, emphasis, facial expressions, etc., what she really is talking about, what he really is saying, what it is that the other really does want. This does not mean her idea is always a good one or she will always agree with his idea, but it does guarantee you will hear and understand what the other is saying. You are then in an honest and intelligent position (mentally and physically) to examine the idea, analyze it, and intelligently express your reaction to it.

The third concept in the rule is and with love. When love is the dominant element in your discussion, you are using the most powerful force known to the human being. You are using God Himself, for "God is love" (I John 4:8). I am talking about the love (the act, the substance, the quality, the way) that God, who is Love, revealed, manifested, shared, and demonstrated toward us — human beings — when we were (and some still are) at odds, antagonistic toward, and eminently in disagreement with the Eternal Heavenly Father, who is Love. When He invites us to "come let us reason together" (Isaiah 1:18), He says that although your disagreements may be blood red like scarlet, they can be made as white as snow, or as white as the wool on a sheep. Reason is one of the qualities of love. But love is more than pure reason. I am talking about a love containing grace (unearned favor) and compassion, "For the Lord is gracious and full of compassion" (Psalms 111:4). I mean a love that is patient, kind, hopeful, has endurance, not jealous or boastful, nor arrogant or rude, does not insist on its own way, does not rejoice or is not happy when the other mate has made a mistake or is wrong. This is a love that never ends, but always wins because it is composed of all the above mental and emotional qualities and is exercised by one loving human being toward another human being.

Fourth, the rule says to talk over anything and everything. All events happening to or involving the couple or family in everyday living — disappointment, sorrow, joy, happiness, hopes, etc. — should be subjects that can be and ought to be discussed by the couple. I do not, of course, include the part of a man or woman's job such as classified military duties or confidential professional services (i.e. what a counselee says, the health of a patient, etc.). These belong to the profession and are privileged and confidential information between doctor and patient, lawyer and client, minister and conferee only. The partner — wife or husband — should not have to be burdened with carrying in their mind and safeguarding such information.

I do not advocate or encourage bringing out the "skeletons from the personal or family closet" that were there prior to the wedding. The subject of the skeletons in the closet should have been thought out and dealt with mentally and emotionally by the individual before marriage. If the individual cannot live with something, then the situation should be discussed before the wedding — not after. The rational mind can forgive and some may forget, but there is a danger of the material being suppressed and deposited in the subconscious mind, which will make use of it in a most effective way, but at the most disastrous times and places.

I do encourage and insist on anything and everything — big or little, good or bad — happening after the wedding are proper subjects for discussion. The closer to the time of the actual occurrence, that actual circumstances permit discussion, before time has made the bad more putrid or rancorous, the better.

The last word in the rule is no less important than what preceeds it: unemotionally. This is without aggression, hostility, anger, or heated arguments. In fact, without arguments at all. The purpose of the conference is not argument, but information, discussion, analysis, understanding, conclusion, and decisions made through love and reason. Why and what makes one become angry? When you get angry, you acknowledge that the situation, obstacle, or object facing you is beyond you. When you are not large enough, strong enough, intelligent enough, and you just cannot cope with, handle, or "lick" the situation or problem with which you are faced, you become angry.

The Answer

What is the difference between being angry with an object or situation and being angry with a person? The difference is that the person is available to argue with or yell at, or even to attack physically. When physical expressions of anger, such as striking a person, are restrained, why do you raise your voice when you are angry and scream or even curse at anyone? Are you not trying to beat down him or her with your loudness and/or profanity? You are trying to employ the "defense mechanism" of force. In marital problems, however, you cannot get the job done by raising your voice and injecting your anger. In fact, anger will not really get the job done on anything. You cannot think rationally (understand, be reasonable) when you are mad. You need to sit down calmly with the other person, present an idea, and talk things over with the best use of your full mental faculties to find the best possible solution that you are both capable of producing.

The popular idea that confronting your spouse when he or she is frustrating you with an aggressive counterattack is completely false. This tactic could reduce your frustration-induced tensions because you have "let off steam," however, at the same time, it will cause so much counter-aggression in your spouse that the entire argument will not make either of you feel any better. The best way to handle such a situation, is to keep your emotions down or out of the picture altogether, approach your spouse in a reasonable manner, and talk over the situation with him or her. Talking is the only effective way to handle frustration.

This is not the place or time for an ego or personality or education contest. That one of you may be a PH.D. and the other only an eighth-grade graduate is not of essential importance. What is important is that each of you honestly gives the best and highest each is capable of in arriving at an equitable and satisfactory solution or answer to the problem at hand. Deal only with the problem at hand. Do not bring into the discussion other problems, past or future, or shortcomings or mistakes or pet peeves. Stick to the context of the subject at hand. That is, deal with one specific problem or situation at a time.

Chapter Thirteen
Creative Ideas

When you sit down to talk things over unemotionally, one of three things will happen. (1) The idea presented is accepted. (2) The original idea is modified. (3) A new idea is created.

When my wife comes in with an idea, no matter how "wild" it may sound on the surface, I have finally, after being married to her for many years, learned to sit down and listen. Suppose she says, "I just saw a new Mercedes-Benz going down the street and, boy, was it a beauty. I think you ought to have one of them to drive instead of that old beat up Volkswagon bus that you drive." Now, my response used to have been, "Woman, are you crazy; completely lost your senses? Where would I get the thousands of dollars needed to buy one?" Now, in reality, I would like to own one of them. When stationed in Germany, sometimes I drove the Mercedes-Benz staff car. It was a real pleasure to cruise along the Autobohn at 70 miles per hour, push a button and do a complete grease job. What a time saver; no waiting at a garage to get the car serviced.

I have not seen my wife since 8:00 a.m. and it is now 4:00 p.m. How do I honestly know what has happened with and to her in that space of time? How do I know whether her rich uncle died and left a million dollars or had struck oil on some land she owns in Texas? How do I know she does not have the money and is about to make me a present of a new Mercedes-Benz? Well, I do not know. So, I say, "Woman, sit down here and tell me what you are talking about." Oh, I did not get the Mercedes-Benz, she did not have the needed money, and I still had the old Volkswagon bus, but it was a nice thought, even if the original idea was not valid. The thought was good because it created a new idea; we pooled our cash, sold the Volkswagen bus, and bought a new (17-foot) Ford motor home — and we paid cash. (This is a true story and the way it really did happen to us.)

As mentioned previously, one of three things will happen when an idea is presented to a husband or wife. You must get your idea formulated and verbalized to give it to your husband and wife. As you make your presentation, you may see the flaws in your ideas for yourself. You soon discover, as you talk, that you really do not want what you are presenting to happen or materialize — the idea was not a good one. At this point you may stop and say, "That simply is not what we want or need, it is not a good idea and it won't work for us." The spouse has not had to say a word; he or she has just been a good listener. Now the spouse can smile understandingly and say nothing or he or she can agree politely, "No, it does not look to me like that is what we would need." Or, the spouse can start a fight or make you feel inches high by saying, "Any 'nitwit' should have known that idea would not work," and push the button on the tape deck and start "The Fight is On, Oh Christian Soldiers" playing.

The second thing that will happen is that as you present the idea, the spouse sees a flaw or hole in the idea. The husband or wife can politely point out the flaw by asking, "Now just what would you do here?" He or she may be able to patch up the hole and go on to present a reasonable, acceptable, and workable idea. Of course, the husband or wife can use the old sledge hammer "defense mechanism" when the flaw is discovered in the idea and say, "Any fool should see that will not work — you've got to do it this way." Thus, the family fight is on!

The third thing that will happen (and within our family, it happens the majority of the time) is a new idea develops and is not the idea that I had or the idea that she had when we sat down to discuss and work on the situation. But, from our sincere and diligent thinking together, a third and better idea has been created. I hasten to say that this is not a compromise, but a third created idea, perhaps related to the first two concepts, but very different, and certainly a better idea for your needs and satisfaction. A compromise is when each gives a little here and takes a little there, reaching something that neither is really proud of or satisfied with, but each of you might manage, by careful and guarded behavior, to live with even though it is really, or maybe definitely, not the answer. Instead, I am talking about a creative idea — created from your best information, intelligence, and logic. In our family, this idea is always better than either of us had when we sat down to talk. This not only will work with husband and wife, but with father, mother, and children sitting down and all of them being allowed, with love and reason, to come and unemotionally construct with the best each has. When all is put together, you have a creative idea belonging to the entire family.

Why are three or six or nine people put on a committee? Why not only one? We have learned through experience that several people can pool their information, know-how, thinking, etc. and construct a better idea than one person. Why does the president announce a dozen or more people for the president's national cabinet? He says they are supposed to advise him, and that would help him find and make better decisions for this nation. That is the principle about which I am speaking. This is what will always happen between a husband and wife who are willing to sit down together and talk unemotionally and creatively over anything and everything. They each give all they have, whether one has a third-grade education and the other has a Ph.D. Their personalities are not competing for prestige, intellect is not competing in an argument for ascendency, energy is not burned up in emotional anger, one is not trying to outdo the other. All the resources of each — common interest, intelligence, information, love, devotion, and just plain common sense and sweat from hard work — have been poured into the problem and an idea, an answer, has been creatively born. The idea is not his or hers, but is "their" idea. It belongs to both of them alike. They both cherish, respond, depend, defend, and act alike upon it. "The two" truly and actually have "become one."

This marriage has found the answer to the mystery of "so they are no longer two but one" (Mark 10:8). Every married couple can find the answer, regardless of their circumstances, nationality, race, religion, creed, education, social standing, or financial standing, if they will use this simple rule —

A WILLINGNESS TO SIT DOWN TOGETHER AND, WITH LOVE, TALK OVER ANYTHING AND EVERYTHING, UNEMOTIONALLY.

No part of this rule can be ignored. Each phrase within this rule is carefully set forth so we can all understand and use this rule. This rule will work — 100% — when it is fully executed.

Chapter Fourteen
The Two Are Now Made One

What has actually happened in this third idea process, or creative decision, is that Tom and Mary have really and truly become one in their thinking, understanding, and agreement. They have actually achieved what Jesus was expressing when he quoted from Genesis 2:24 in Mark 10:8, "And the two shall become one."

It is generally accepted and agreed that one's actions and behavior come from and are controlled by one's thinking and beliefs, "For as he thinketh in his heart, so is he" (Proverbs 23:7). If the two of you sit down together and create your ideas by pouring yourselves totally, all you have, into the idea, it will be, as said before, "your idea," not hers or his, but "YOURS." Now that the idea belongs alike to both of you, each one will act alike on the idea. You will, therefore, act in one way, not two different ways. In other words, you two — husband and wife — literally act in unison or act as one. When others deal with the wife, they would have the same result as if they had dealt with the husband on any given situation or idea that had been thus created by them as "their idea." Hence, your actions become one to the community. You stand together as a family and the community knows this and can depend on where you stand on various questions and issues.

Your children will not grow up neurotic, trying to decide who is right and which parent to mind, respect, and receive instruction. The poor children will no longer be left out in the middle of the room with Mother in one corner and Father in the other corner and the children emotionally, psychologically, and logically torn between which parent to listen to or agree with because the two of you are not saying the same thing either by word or action. When husband and wife have "become one," the children's confusion cannot and does not exist. Neither can children become the victims of a broken home, as so many are today, if Father and Mother are "one" because there could be no divorce or legal separation when the "two are one."

Now that both of you have come to understand this new human relationship and the uniqueness of the marriage bond, you are willing to sit down together and talk over anything and everything unemotionally, thereby creatively constructing "your ideas," which will not only guide and direct your thinking and behavior, but will give consistent, reliable, dependable, acceptable, and wholesome guidance to your children. This kind of home produces an atmosphere of love, understanding, appreciation, and security. Therefore, this home is not a mill for producing and turning out neurotic personalities or hippies or yippies or dope addicts or alcoholics or just plain criminals for children. The children of your home will not be numbered among the estimated millions of school-aged children in the United States needing, but not getting, mental and emotional professional help because there are not enough psychiatrists and psychologists to take care of these extra millions over the ones presently receiving treatment. The two of you have become "one" and are not ambivalent or contradictory in your ideas and behavior. This situation not only has produced a secure and stable home for the wholesome physical, mental, emotional, moral, and spiritual development for the children, but has produced a home recognized and acknowledged as respectable and is an influence with power and force for stabilization and good for the community in which you and your children live.

I have set forth, from my experiences and research, my theories and beliefs on the concept of marriage as a "unique, but not mysterious, human experience" and "the two becoming one," not as allegory, but as actual, literal, lovable, harmonious, and behavioral fact.

The basic question, as stated previously, that set me on this search in the marriage field, was "Why and how could my wife, and no other woman in the whole wide world, affect me as she could by leaving me standing in the middle of the floor as if my feet were nailed to the floor, my hands were tied to my side, my mouth was sealed, and a little blue blaze was coming out of the top of my head?" I had to find the answer for myself to my own satisfaction. Happily, I have found that answer to my own satisfaction. Out of this answer is the basis upon which the theories I have presented are founded.

The most direct and short answer to this question that I can give is: I am married to her — she is my wife. Marriage is a unique human experience; unique because there is no other experience like it. This experience is different from any other human relationship and, therefore, must be handled and dealt with in a different way than other personal relationships. The marriage relationship is unique, but not mysterious because marriage is understandable. When something can be explained and understood, there is no mystery about it. Since Bonnie Ruth and I have come to understand the uniqueness of marriage, there is no mystery about it for us. We learned that marriage operates under a different set of rules than other human relationships. Marriage is not subject to and cannot operate successfully to any degree by the use of the two "defense mechanisms" of "avoidance" and "force," the natural defenses known to and used by human beings from birth to death and used by every living thing on this earth that breathes and moves.

The reason why Bonnie Ruth cannot now affect me, nor I affect her, as we did for the first 20 years of our marriage is because we have now learned to know how to respond better to each other. We have learned the marriage relationship is unique and this relationship operates under an entirely new set of rules. In other words, our old "defense mechanisms" of avoidance and force are entirely and completely ineffectual in our marriage relationship. In fact, although we did not know it, they became null and void the day we took the marriage vows, for any relationship between us, even though we used them on every other human relationship — kin, friend, or foe. Therefore, Bonnie Ruth is no longer "that woman" to me because I have learned she is my WIFE. I am no longer "that man" to her because she has learned I am her HUSBAND. When I discovered and realized that, after we were married, Bonnie Ruth did not act like my mother, or my sister, or even as she did when she was my girl friend before we were married, or like any other female whom I had known because she could not since she was none of these, but is my wife — and she could only act in that capacity and manner — she ceased to be "that woman" because she was my wife. Her relationship to me could only be as a wife because that was what she had voluntarily become to me through the marriage vows when we took each other "to have and to hold from this day forward, for better, for worse, for richer, for poorer, in sickness and in health, to love and to cherish, 'till death us do part.'"

I have illustrated the different relationships that we encounter by use of the charts previously drawn. I feel it is a good explanation for understanding why the husband-wife relationship is unique. It may be helpful to go back and study these charts again. All human relationships, EXCEPT the marital relationship, are handled by the two "defense mechanisms" of "avoidance" and "force." The vertical lines of the chart represent relationships that respond, to a more or less successful degree, to these "defense mechanisms." The horizontal line represents the marital relationship, which cannot to any degree respond to these "defense mechanisms."

Nonetheless, why has no other women ever affected me as Bonnie Ruth could and did for the first 20 years of our marriage? Those other women were not, and never have been, my wife. They were just other females in the roles of mother, sister, girl friend, or stranger whose relationships I dealt with, in success or failure, through the use of my old "defense mechanisms" of avoidance and force.

If Bonnie Ruth had been wife number 3, rather than the only woman to whom I have ever been married, then wife number 1 and wife number 2 would each have affected me the same way Bonnie Ruth was able to affect me during the first 20 years that we were married. Now she can no longer do this because I have learned better. I know she is my wife and she must and does act in her relationship to me as a wife and not as any other woman.

If you are living with husband number 5 and do not know what to do with him or how to deal with him, you really cannot understand what makes "that man" tick; if he can make you fighting mad and cause you to explode into a fit of anger over a little bit of nothing; if he can leave you, as it were, standing in the middle of the room as if your feet were nailed to the floor, your hands were tied to your sides, your mouth was taped shut, and a little blue blaze was coming out of the top of your head, then you have not yet learned he is your husband, the marriage relationship is unique and, therefore, different from any other human relationship, and your marriage relationship must be handled by a new and different set of rules than those with which you have reacted to and dealt with all other human beings, male or female.

If husband number 5 can and does affect you that way, so did husbands number 1, 2, 3, and 4. That is really why you are now married to and living with husband number 5. If you will let your mind go back and look at and analyze the past situations, you will discover the five husbands to whom you were married (not men with whom you just voluntarily domiciled — they did not affect you that way because you were not married to them) all affected you very much the same way, but differently from the hundreds of other male human beings that you know and deal with as relatives, business associates, social companions, friends, or just casual strangers. You dealt with all of these others through your regular, natural "defense mechanisms" of avoidance and force. But you cannot use these "defense mechanisms" of avoidance and force on your husband and have a home. If you pick up your dolls and go home to Mother, you do not have a home. If you start fighting with your husband (physically, mentally, or morally) with fist, tongue, or attitude, you create a "living hell" and not a home.

I have said all this before, but because it is imperative and absolutely necessary that a husband and a wife realize and understand marriage IS unique and the marrige relationship CANNOT respond to the normal "defense mechanisms" of avoidance and force to any degree and still exist within an happy and successfully stable home for both the couple and the children. Time and again I have repeated these ideas and concepts, hoping thereby to help you mentally and emotionally to assimilate and lay hold of the truth of them and to help you put these principles to immediate use. Although simple, these principles are difficult to employ and execute in dealing with a wife or a husband (because of the way we have handled all other human experiences) to create a happy and successful marriage and a home for the rearing of normal, stable, well-adjusted children.

The home is the basic of all human institutions — religious, educational, scientific, economic, or governmental. The whole quality of human life on this earth has its roots in the home. The kind and quality of homes created by us determines the quality of life for all human beings. Whether our homes reflect the quality of "a heaven" or a "living hell" depends on the kind and quality of the marital relationship between the husband and wife. Therefore, it is very important to recognize that marriage is unique — no other experience is like it — but not mysterious because marriage can be explained and understood. For God created human beings "in His own image, male and female created He them. And God blessed them and said, be fruitful and multiply and replenish the earth" (Genesis 1:27-28). And I would add in harmony, peace, and happiness, which are yours for the taking since you now know how to create and receive them.

Chapter Fifteen
Another Phase

There is, of course, what might be called another phase of the marital problem, which we have not discussed, but is of equal importance. We cannot ignore the possibility of human error, sin, and temptation or their results and effects on the human life. Men and women are tempted and sometimes they yield, as the old hymn says, "Yield not to temptation, for yielding is sin." We cannot ignore the patterns of thought, philosophy, moral and religious training, habits formed and personality developed in a man or a woman in the years prior to their marriage. We have to begin with them where they are when they come to the wedding day, scars and warts or roses and tulips — "for better, for worse" — as they really are.

Before marriage, there has been a great deal of living already done. There is often subconscious aggression from childhood experiences and hurts as well as consciously remembered experiences and hurts that have influenced the thinking, habits, and behavior of the individual subconsciously as well as consciously to be discovered and dealt with by the newly acquired companion through the institution of marriage. Often there are many wounds to be healed and much aggression, animosity, bitterness, etc. needing to be emptied from a husband or wife that have accumulated before the marriage. Just standing before the altar of a church or temple or legal authority and saying "I do" in a wedding ceremony, or signing a legal marriage contract will not be sufficient to take care of and render void these formerly acquired undesirable attitudes, habits, thoughts, and behaviors. Therefore, the basic theory and approach used by me for many years in this phase of marriage could basically be summed up in one sentence from the teaching of Jesus, as recorded in the Holy Bible by St. Paul in Romans 12:21, "Overcome evil with good." Conciously, the evil, bitterness, aggression, and undesirable are flushed out and replaced with the beautiful, good, and desirable. The basic and proven psychological principles and methods in applying the general principles of Jesus' teaching, "Overcome evil with good," form the basic concepts and methods used by me.

When one is filled with aggression and bitterness, one is often tormented by a guilt feeling and begins to punish oneself by beating oneself over the head, so to speak. However, no amount of self-bludgeoning can remove the aggression or bitterness from the inside of an individual. Some people try to get rid of guilt by the "vacuum pump" method — mentally and emotionally sucking and pulling at the guilt. The effect of this vacuum method is that it tends to draw off one's energy and efficiency until a physical or emotional or mental breakdown puts one in the hospital or a mental ward because nature abhors a vacuum and life cannot tolerate it. The aggression and bitterness (guilt) must be flushed out and replaced with something more desirable and useful — the good, beautiful, happy, life-sustaining values of a positive and well-adjusted person — that is, "Overcome evil with good."

With an ordinary empty paper cup, this principle can be effectively demonstrated. In counseling a person with these problems (whether married or unmarried), to help them grasp the truth of overcoming evil with

Another Phase

good, I pick up an ordinary paper drinking cup, hold it with the open end toward the individual, and ask, "With what is this cup filled?" Always, the answer is, "Nothing, it is empty." "But," I insist, "it is full of the air in this room." To this the person will readily agree. How can we ge the air out of the paper cup? We could take this book and smash it flat, but that would destroy the cup. Then, I suggest we could take a vacuum pump and suck out the air, but before I have time to go through with it, my counselee says, "But the cup will collapse. It is not strong enough to withstand a vacuum." I agree, the counselee is absolutely correct. This is exactly the problem that an individual has with herself or himself in eliminating aggressing, bitterness, and guilt down in the heart and subconscious mind.

Nonetheless, the answer to removing the air from the paper cup is so simple that a small child can accomplish it. A child can take this cup over to the water faucet and fill it with pure, clear, clean water and the water will displace the air in the cup. Thus, getting rid of aggression, bitterness, and guilt, is just as simple — flush it out with the good. You have got to fill the "cup" of your life and not destroy it because the undesirable and harmful have gotten into your "cup of life." "Overcome evil with good."

How do you overcome evil with good? The answer — by conscious thought. Fill the conscious and subconscious mind with "the good" through positive thoughts, faith in yourself, faith in God, prayer, and belief. "If thou canst believe, all things are possible to him that believeth" (Mark 9:23). As the ancient Hebrew proverb says, "For as he thinketh in his heart, so is he" (Proverbs 23:7).

I use what I call my "Spiritual Prescriptions." (I used to work in a drug store as a pharmacist, filling doctors' prescriptions for healing people's ills.) These Spiritual Prescriptions are for the same purpose — healing people's ills in mind, soul, and body. As an example, I often prescribed Joshua 1:9, "Be strong and of a good courage; be not afraid, neither be thou dismayed: for the Lord thy God is with thee whithersoever thou goest"; or I would give Isaiah 40:31, "But they that wait upon the Lord shall renew their strength; they shall mount up with wings as eagles; they shall run, and not be weary; and they shall walk, and not faint"; or Philippians 4:13, "I can do all things through Christ which strengtheneth me." Sometimes I prescribed Psalm 55:22, "Cast thy burden upon the Lord, and he shall sustain thee," or Romans 8:31, "If God be for us, who can be against us?" and many more life giving principles of the many the Holy Bible has for the solution to every human need.

The directions for using these prescriptions were simple — memorize or write down the verse on a card and read or say it thoughtfully many times during the day. For special effectiveness, repeat the verse thoughtfully and deeply as you drop off to sleep so it will sink into your subconscious mind. This will happen as surely as a book pushed off the edge of a desk will fall to the floor. Do these things for a period of seven days. The cycle of seven is important, for some mysterious reason. For instance, all known calendars of time have seven days in a week. They may differ in the number of days in the month or the number of months in the year, but all have seven days in the week. Seven seems to be related to the nature and order of things on this planet Earth.

Another Phase

You cannot go to sleep while you are thinking and worrying about anything. You have to get it off your mind, either by conscious effort or by sheer physical exhaustion, before you can fall asleep. The last five minutes before you go to sleep are the most important five minutes of your day. If you can consciously lay aside and clear your mind of the worries and problems of the day and serenely and peacefully go to sleep, well and good. However, if through pure physical exhaustion you finally drop off to sleep — usually a fitful and restless sleep — then the worries, problems, hatred, anger, animosity, bitterness, or fear on your mind has been dropped from your conscious into your subconscious.

Your subconscious mind will take whatever YOU give it, good or bad, and will work continuously with the material and hand it back to your conscious mind in the shortest and most effective way possible from time to time. These thoughts are then influencing and directing your conscious actions, behavior, and attitudes for good or bad, depending on what you have given your subconscious to work with. You need to select your thoughts deliberately and intentionally. The more emotional content or feeling that you put into them, the more effective they are. You may consciously examine and try to evaluate and understand your actions or behavior on certain occasions or in given situations, and all the answer you can find is "Why? Why did I say or do that? Why did I get angry? Why did I act that way? Why? Why?" The only answer you can honestly get is, "I don't know. I should not have acted that way. I did not intend to say such things, they just popped out — why?" The real answer is your subconscious mind has handed back to your conscious mind what you have been storing up there.

How can you get rid of these undesirable materials of hatred, anger, animosity, aggression, bitterness, and fear? Use the principle set forth by St. Paul in his letter to the Romans, "Be not overcome of evil, but overcome evil with good." In other words, consciously flush out of the subconscious mind all the undesirable materials (hatred, bitterness, anger, animosity, aggression, fear, etc.) that you have stored up (in your deeper self of heart, mind, and emotions) by consciously putting into the subconscious the desirable materials (the good, beautiful, joyful, wholesome, courageous, peaceful, loving, faithful, happy, etc.). These help make us a personality that you, yourself, as well as others — your wife or husband — can respect and love. You can do it, and if you will ask Him, "My God shall supply all your need according to his riches in glory by Christ Jesus" (Philippians 4:19).

The words of the Bible do relate to all human situations, good or bad. The Bible's words can be used for the mental and spiritual healing and health of anyone who will use them. The words of the Bible are alive. In fact, the Bible itself states, "If you abide in me, and my words abide in you, you shall ask what you will, and it shall be done unto you" (John 15:17). This is why I use Scripture verses as Spiritual Prescriptions for mental, emotional, and spiritual health.

Displacement is the only method whereby you can drive out a thought from your mind. To select words from the Bible (verses), memorize them, repeat them over and over many times each day (fill the conscious mind with positive words) will not only help direct your thoughts from the negative to the positive things during

Another Phase

your day, but these powerful spiritual words will sink from your conscious to your subconscious mind by a seepage or spiritual osmosis, therefore, changing your negative personality, giving you spiritual power, and making you more positive and receptive to God's will in your life. You can and will become a more respected and lovable person, even to yourself. (If you do not respect and love yourself, how can you except or receive respect and love for others? As the Reverend Dr. Robert Schuller says, "If you don't love yourself, it is time you repent.") You will be "overcoming evil with good" by the method or process of displacement — flushing out the undesirable and bad with the desirable and good.

Week after week your conscious and subconscious minds will be filled with positive words of power, sensitivity to God's operation in your life, and greater value of this life for you. These powerful positive words from the Bible will displace your negative, unhappy, and unhealthy thoughts as you develop a more dynamic personality. You will become a better companion, husband or wife, and parent to your children.

Perhaps you are skeptical and have some doubts about the value of the above described method for displacing your negative thoughts with selected positive words from the Bible and emptying your subconscious mind of undesirable material by flushing or driving it out with these positive words. Perhaps you feel you are above us average sinners and you are a well adjusted man or woman (married or single) and you have no real need of any psychological or spiritual help. Then I challenge you — in fact, dare you — to try the following experiment conscientiously, sincerely, and honestly for seven consecutive days.

Read Psalm 23 from the Holy Bible sincerely, thoughtfully, and meditatively five times each day for seven consecutive days. Do not recite from memory, but thoughtfully and meditatively read aloud as you look at each printed word. By reading aloud from the printed text, you are receivng the message through three different avenues — your mind, your eyes, and your ears. This is important to the experiment. The time of day when you read is also important; no variation of times or method is tolerated for the full seven days.

> First reading: When you get up in the morning.
> Second reading: Before breakfast. If you are one of those people not eating breakfast, read at the time you normally should eat a good breakfast.
> Third reading: At noon, before you eat your lunch.
> Fourth reading: At supper time, before you eat your meal.
> Fifth reading: When you retire, as the last thing before you go to sleep.

I should warn you, if you are completely satisfied with yourself just as you are, and definitely do not want any change in yourself to take place, then DO NOT sincerely and honestly carry out and complete this experiment, because you will be opening yourself to the risk of change. Your spouse, children, business associates, and friends may even detect the changes — but they will like what they see!

About the Author

Melvin Ray Miller began his life's work as a teacher, student counselor, and administrator in the public school system of Oklahoma and later in Texas. He was licensed to preach by The Methodist Episcopal Church, South, in 1926 and became a full-time pastor in 1930. On May 18 of that year he was married to Bonnie Ruth Mains, a classroom teacher.

In the course of his ministry, Rev. Miller served pastorates in Oklahoma, Texas, and North Carolina. Although retired from the active ministry of The United Methodist Church in 1970, he notes: "The Lord has not retired me yet. I am now only as old as Moses was when he started to lead the children of Israel out of Egypt. In order to equal Moses' record before the Lord retired him, I will have to serve 40 more years!"

For 22 years Rev. Miller served with the Armed Forces of the United States, 20 of those years spent in the role of chaplain. He was retired from the Air Force in 1965 with the rank of Lt. Colonel.

For over 58 years, Rev. Miller has been recognized for his outstanding success in his field, expecially during the last 35 years of his career which have been concentrated in Premarital, Marriage and Family life counseling. During this extended period, Rev. Miller's military assignments and ministerial duties have carried him into each of the 50 states of the union, as well as into 38 other nations on four continents. He has thus had the opportunity for first-hand observation and study of the cultural and social patterns, educational systems, religious and secular training, personality traits, and particularly the marriage customs and relationships of many nationalities, races, and creeds.

In addition to the broad perspective gained through his extensive travel and career opportunities, Rev. Miller has maintained an active interest in academic and professional studies, earning the B.A., B.D. and M. Div. degrees and completing additional graduate work in personal counseling, psychotherapy and clinical psychology.

Rev. and Mrs. Miller now reside in Florida.